A HISTORY OF THE AMERICAN CARDINALS DINNER
at The Catholic University
of America

Martin J. Moran

Martin J. Moran

FIRST EDITION

Copyright 2016 by Martin J. Moran

Martin J. Moran, Post Office Box 53, Massapequa
Park, New York 11762

Printed in the United States of America

ISBN Number: 978-0-9834617-1-5

Library of Congress Control Number: 2015901161

Photo on cover:

*An aerial view of the Catholic University's main
campus from the Knights' Tower of the Basilica of the
National Shrine of the Immaculate Conception.*

TABLE OF CONTENTS

President John Garvey

FOREWORD BY

CUA PRESIDENT JOHN GARVEY

A t The 26th American Cardinals Dinner, senior politics major Kaitlynn O'Leary addressed the audience with these words: "It occurred to me, while we were physically helping to put up the structure of a house [for Habitat for Humanity], that this alone did not make it a home. It is the loving and caring people inside the house that truly make a place a home. Over the past four years, I am proud to say that The Catholic University of America has become my home. I know even after I graduate, thanks to your generous support, that this will forever be a place for me to return to."

Kaitlynn, like hundreds of other Catholic University students, was able to take advantage of the exceptional educational experience this university offers because of the scholarship aid that was raised over the 26-year history of this remarkable dinner. Who could have imagined back in the late 1980s, when Smith Bagley and the Board of Regents dreamed of a dinner where all the American Cardinals would come together in support of Catholic University students, that we would raise more than $33.5 million in scholarship funds?

As you read this history of the American cardinals dinner you will be reminded how this university is inextricably linked to the Catholic Church, and even more, how Church leaders have strongly supported us since our inception. I am grateful to Martin Moran for taking on this project that chronicles the history of the cardinals dinner and integrates significant aspects of the university's history in telling the story. I am also grateful to the members of the university staff and faculty who assisted in this effort. In a very special way I want to thank my predecessors, Rev. William Byron, S.J., Brother Patrick Ellis, F.S.C., and Bishop David O'Connell, C.M., who met with Marty and gave so generously of their valuable time to ensure the accuracy of this history.

Perhaps most important, I want to thank the thousands of benefactors who gave so generously to make the American cardinals dinners so unique, entertaining, and successful in every possible way. It has been my honor to join with the cardinals and host bishops in celebrating these dinners.

John Garvey
President
The Catholic University of America

MISSION STATEMENT

As the national university of the Catholic Church in the United States, founded and sponsored by the bishops of the country with the approval of the Holy See, The Catholic University of America is committed to being a comprehensive Catholic and American institution of higher learning, faithful to the teachings of Jesus Christ as handed on by the Church. Dedicated to advancing the dialogue between faith and reason, The Catholic University of America seeks to discover and impart the truth through excellence in teaching and research, all in service to the Church, the nation, and the world.

The Flagship Catholic University

The Catholic University of America is unique as the national university of the Catholic Church and as the only higher education institution founded by the U.S. bishops. Established in 1887 as a papally chartered graduate and research center, the university began offering undergraduate education in 1904.

Caldwell Hall, the first new building on campus. Cardinal James Gibbons presided at the laying of the building's cornerstone in 1888, with President Grover Cleveland in attendance.

PRESIDENTS OF
THE CATHOLIC UNIVERSITY OF AMERICA

Bishop John J. Keane
1887–1896

Bishop Thomas J. Conaty
1896–1903

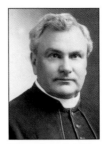

Bishop Denis J. O'Connell
1903–1909

Bishop Thomas J. Shahan
1909–1927

Bishop James Hugh Ryan
1928–1935

Bishop Joseph M. Corrigan
1936–1942

Bishop Patrick J. McCormick
1943–1953

Bishop Bryan J. McEntegart
1953–1957

Bishop William J. McDonald
1957–1967

Clarence C. Walton
1969–1978

Edmund D. Pellegrino,
M.D., 1978–1982

Reverend William J. Byron,
S.J., 1982–1992

Brother Patrick Ellis, F.S.C.
1992–1998

Bishop David M. O'Connell
C.M., 1998–2010

John Garvey
2010–Present

CHANCELLORS OF
THE CATHOLIC UNIVERSITY OF AMERICA

Cardinal James Gibbons
Archbishop of Baltimore
CUA Chancellor
1887–1921

Archbishop Michael J. Curley
Archbishop of Baltimore
CUA Chancellor
1921–1947

Patrick Cardinal O'Boyle
Archbishop of Washington
CUA Chancellor
1948–1973

Cardinal William Baum
Archbishop of Washington
CUA Chancellor
1973–1980

Cardinal James Hickey
Archbishop of Washington
CUA Chancellor
1980–2000

Cardinal Theodore McCarrick
Archbishop of Washington
CUA Chancellor
2000–2006

Cardinal Donald Wuerl
Archbishop of Washington
CUA Chancellor
2006–Present

INTRODUCTION

INTRODUCTION

A History of The American Cardinals Dinner

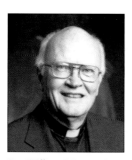

Rev. William J. Byron, S.J.

Brother Patrick Ellis, F.S.C.

Bishop David M. O'Connell, C.M.

John Garvey

This is a chronological history of the 26 years of the American Cardinals Dinner, which The Catholic University of America began holding in December 1989. The silver anniversary dinner was held in May 2014 and the 26th in April 2015.

The dinner was planned to be a yearly event as a tribute to American cardinals who are diocesan bishops for the benefit of scholarships at The Catholic University of America. The dinners were also intended to recognize United States cardinals who are retired, who serve the Church in the Vatican, and, on occasion, cardinals visiting from another country.

The location of the dinner rotated to a different city each year, beginning with dioceses served by a cardinal and eventually to dioceses headed by clerical members of the Catholic University Board of Trustees. A key purpose of the dinners was to enhance the visibility of the university in all parts of America.

The First American Cardinals Dinner was the concluding event of Catholic University's centennial ceremonies. The dinners were held yearly until 2016. A narrative and pictorial history of each of these gala functions will be reviewed here along with a wide variety of other notable events and a description of the extraordinary physical development of the university campus from 1989 to 2015.

The president of The Catholic University of America cohosted the cardinals dinner with the highest-ranking member of the clergy of the host city. During the period covered here, the cohosting president was a Jesuit priest for three years, a La Salle brother for six, a Vincentian priest for 12, and a layman since 2011.

Four different presidents led The Catholic

University of America during this period. Rev. William J. Byron, S.J., kicked off the university's centennial on Founders Day, April 10, 1987, and concluded the proceedings with The First American Cardinals Dinner on December 12, 1989. Succeeding presidents — Brother Patrick Ellis, F.S.C., Very Rev. David M. O'Connell, C. M., and John Garvey — continued the gala dinners each year thereafter. President Garvey led the celebration of the 125th anniversary of the university on Founders Day, April 10, 2012. The 25th American Cardinals Dinner was held in May 2014 with Cardinal Timothy Dolan and President Garvey cohosting this silver anniversary event in New York City.

Pope Leo XIII signed the papal decree in 1887 creating Catholic University.

The Catholic University of America Founded in 1887

A Plenary Council is a national meeting of Roman Catholic bishops, convened to discuss matters relevant to the governance of the American church and to foster common discipline. During the 19th century there were three such councils, all held in Baltimore. The Third Plenary Council of bishops met there from November 9 to December 7, 1884, led by Archbishop James Gibbons of Baltimore, with 14 archbishops, 61 bishops, six abbots, and one superior general of a religious congregation in attendance. Its decrees were presented for approval to Pope Leo XIII. Among them was a proposal that a Catholic university be created. The Holy Father agreed and the initial steps toward the founding of The Catholic University of America were under way.

A Pontifical Charter was issued on April 10, 1887, the cornerstone for Caldwell Hall was laid in 1888, and The Catholic University of America was officially opened on November 13, 1889, timed to coincide with the centennial of the naming of John Carroll as the first United States bishop in November 1789. The Pope stated that the university was to be "under the authority and

Some Decrees from the 1884 Plenary Council

- The bishops agreed to petition the Holy See to establish The Catholic University of America, which received its papal charter in 1887.

- The Baltimore Catechism was published, containing all tenets of the Church, in question-and-answer form. This was the basis of Catholic religious instruction for the next 100 years.

- Each parish was required to establish an elementary school. This set in motion the system of Catholic parochial schools from coast to coast.

- This council determined that all Catholics observe six holy days of obligation, a decree that has basically held steady to today.

protection of all the bishops of the country" and so it remains. In his 1887 papal charter, Pope Leo stipulated that intellectual excellence be the university's aim.

Catholic University and the Cardinals of the United States

The cardinals of the United States and The Catholic University of America have enjoyed a close relationship since the university's creation. Cardinal James Gibbons of Baltimore, the only United States cardinal at the time, was a principal proponent of the university and presided at the groundbreaking ceremonies. Since that time each cardinal resident in the United States has been a member of the governing body of the university.

On November 6, 1789, the same year that George Washington was sworn in as president of the United States, the Pope issued a papal brief creating the Diocese of Baltimore. In November of 1889, exactly 100 years later, the first students arrived on the campus of The Catholic University

Cardinal James Gibbons, archbishop of Baltimore, endorsed the creation of CUA and was chancellor from 1887 to 1921.

of America in Washington, D.C. The First American Cardinals Dinner, held in December 1989, therefore, was a celebration not only of the centennial of Catholic University, but also of the bicentennial of the establishment of the Church in the United States.

The cornerstone for Caldwell Hall was laid in 1888, with the official opening of the university in November 1889. President Grover Cleveland attended the cornerstone celebration and President Benjamin Harrison the formal opening. Over the years,

Catholic University has maintained its unique status as the only American university having ecclesiastical ties to the Holy See and to the hierarchy of the United States, while belonging to and receiving support from all Catholics of the nation.

From this brief summary of the foundation of the university, the next section transitions to the second half of the 10-year tenure of its 12th president, Rev. William J. Byron, S.J., who presided over the Catholic University centennial celebration in 1987 and convened The First American Cardinals Dinner two years later.

Historic McMahon Hall, constructed in 1895.

CHAPTER ONE

CHAPTER ONE

Reverend William J. Byron, S.J.
Catholic University President
1982–1992

ev. William J. Byron, S.J., became the 12th president of The Catholic University of America in September 1982. For the prior seven years he was president of the University of Scranton and, before that, dean of arts and sciences at Loyola College of Baltimore (now Loyola University of Maryland). A Jesuit, he was the first member of a religious order to lead Catholic University.

A native of Pittsburgh, Father Byron was raised in Philadelphia, where he graduated from St. Joseph's Preparatory School and joined the United States Army, becoming a member of the 508th Parachute Infantry Regiment. Following military service, he attended Saint Joseph's University in Philadelphia before entering the Society of Jesus, and was ordained in 1961. In 1969 he received a doctorate in economics from the University of Maryland. He also had two theology degrees from Woodstock College and a bachelor's degree in philosophy and master's in economics from Saint Louis University.

From 1982 to 1992, Father Byron led Catholic University to new heights academically as well as in dramatic improvement and development of the physical campus. In 1986 as the university was preparing to commemorate the Catholic University centennial, Father Byron created a Board of Regents to assist with matters relating to the general welfare of the university, financial matters, and public relations. More than 40 prominent men and women from all parts of the nation were brought together, a group that included corporate, civic, and religious leaders, many of whom had no previous association with the university. The idea of having an American Cardinals Dinner came from this group who, with Father Byron's encouragement and support, carried it forward with vigor and success.

During Father Byron's decade as president, he

Rev. William J. Byron, S.J.

completed $51 million in construction projects, including the creation of a new athletic complex, the Raymond A. DuFour Athletic Center, on North Campus and expansion of undergraduate university housing with Centennial Village, named for the university's 100th anniversary. He tripled the endowment and began fund-raising to build a new law school.

Father Byron was awarded the Cardinal Gibbons Medal by Catholic University in 1991. At the dedication of the new Columbus School of Law in the fall of 1994, the Rev. William J. Byron, S. J. Auditorium there was named in his honor.

During the fall of 1986, Father Byron announced plans for a three-year series of ceremonies commemorating the first 100 years of the national Catholic university. The formal kick-off dinner took place on Founders Day, April 10, 1987, and the festivities ended with The First American Cardinals Dinner on December 12, 1989. George W. Bush, the 41st president of the United States, spoke at both the centennial kick-off dinner, when he was vice president, and at The First American Cardinals Dinner, when he was president.

At the dinner, Bush said, "I often hear that you can't teach values, but Catholic University is living proof that you can. The Catholic University of America has prided itself for the past century on providing students with solid ideals based on a firm foundation of morals, values and ethics. This sense and purpose sets Catholic University apart from many other institutions in this great country. We need Catholic University's voice and commitment to the minds and souls of our young people."

The Catholic University of America Transformed

The initial cardinals dinner marked the beginning of dramatic transformations over the next 25 years at Catholic University. The accomplishments over this period, under four administrations, have been truly astonishing. The commitment of the university to vastly improving the quality of

President and Mrs. George H.W. Bush are greeted by Father William J, Byron, S.J., and Cardinal James Hickey at The First American Cardinals Dinner in December 1989. President Bush was the principal speaker at both this dinner and, as vice president, at the Catholic University centennial kick-off celebration in 1987.

Gibbons Hall
Named for CUA's first chancellor, Cardinal James Gibbons, this century-old building was renovated in 1988. The funds for its construction came from donations given to the cardinal in the celebration of the 50th anniversary of his ordination. Gibbons was archbishop of Baltimore from 1877 to 1921 and named a cardinal in 1886; he died in 1921. Cardinal Gibbons blessed the cornerstone in 1888 and a year later dedicated Gibbons Hall.

The Raymond A. DuFour Athletic Center, dedicated in September 1986.

student life has been mirrored by many and varied academic accomplishments, with special emphasis placed on embracing and exhibiting the fact that The Catholic University of America was truly "Catholic" in every way.

The most evident changes during the period between the first and 26th American Cardinals Dinner were the visible transformation of the campus itself.

■ Fifteen new buildings were constructed and almost all existing facilities completely renovated and/or dramatically refurbished.

■ The significant improvements to the DuFour Center complex on North Campus provide the student body with a wide array of athletic and recreational opportunities.

■ All student residences were located north of Michigan Avenue with new student construction in close proximity to athletic and recreational facilities.

■ A new 49-acre West Campus was acquired.

■ The nine-acre South Campus was transformed into a mixed-use complex of residential units, retail shops, and a variety of other business and cultural entities.

■ Hundreds of new shrubs, flowers, and trees were planted in all parts of the property.

The American Cardinals Dinner

The idea to have an American Cardinals Dinner came from the Catholic University Board of Regents, which had a variety of roles, one of them to raise funds for the university. It was understood that each regent would "give or get" $10,000 per year for the university. Those who had the financial ability could simply write a check. Most regents found that difficult. They had to give some and get their friends, family members, business associates, or others to contribute the remainder.

When the regents elected Smith Bagley as second chairman, they found a leader with substantial financial resources and experience in raising funds, who took the job of chairman very seriously. He was an heir to the R. J. Reynolds family tobacco fortune, a major donor to and worker for the National Democratic Committee, and known around Washington as "a man who got things done." He also knew how to get others to raise money for a cause. Bagley considered raising funds for a worthwhile cause like Catholic University much easier than for a political party or a political figure. Contributions to the university were tax deductible, as opposed to political causes, which were not, and for those in the habit of giving each year to many charities, this was important. From experience, he also knew that a "vehicle" was needed for donors to rally around.

Bagley suggested that Catholic University have a major event, like a dinner, as the vehicle for the Board of Regents to take ownership of and to which their friends and associates could be asked to contribute. As a convert, becoming a Catholic when he married Elizabeth Frawley several years earlier, Bagley was not very conversant with the organization of the Catholic Church, but he knew that there was something special about cardinals. In his view, they were the royalty of the Church, the "top bananas." He reasoned that the intimate involvement of United States cardinals in an annual event for the national Catholic university would place the Board of Regents in a position to have a successful enterprise. Having regents from all parts of the country, Bagley felt this event would give them a project they could rally around and he knew they would not be averse to rubbing shoulders with American cardinals.

At a spring 1989 board meeting he offered the idea of concluding the centennial and beginning the second century of The Catholic University of America with a gala $1,000-a-plate American cardinals dinner. His vision was to have a major black-tie event each year, in a city where a local cardinal resided, cohosted by the university president and the local archbishop. The dinner itself, in addition to being a social event, was intended to attract attention to the university and recruit new, top caliber undergraduate and graduate students from all parts of the country. The dinners would raise new money each year to provide generous scholarship grants to many who might otherwise not be able to afford to attend

Catholic University, thereby providing the gift of an education to many who were in need. He wanted to raise everyone's sights by having $1,000 be the price of each dinner ticket, an amount unheard of for an institution like The Catholic University of America in 1989. Bagley suggested to the Board of Regents that he was making it easier for each of them to fulfill their annual requirement to raise $10,000 for Catholic University. A regent, simply by taking responsibility for one table, would fulfill the commitment. A regent attending with his spouse or friend would have to sell only another eight tickets to produce the requirement.

A number of preliminary steps had to fall into place before the selling of tickets could begin. Smith Bagley sold the idea to the Board of Regents and board moderator, Monsignor William A. Kerr, vice president for university relations. Monsignor Kerr and Bagley convinced Father Byron who convinced the Board of Trustees, including Cardinal James Hickey, archbishop of Washington and Catholic University chancellor. Cardinal Hickey secured the agreement of each of the other cardinals, some of whom agreed to attend the first dinner, without committing to the future.

Once the first dinner in Washington had the go-ahead, Bagley very quickly secured a handsome site, the magnificently renovated historic Pension Building in downtown Washington, D.C. Now known as the National Building Museum, its interesting history would in itself be a "draw." Bagley and the committee agreed that the dinner would be held early in December each year. Although he liked the idea of setting a precise annual date it had to be scrubbed as impractical considering the number of individual schedules that had to be accommodated.

Indeed, right from the start setting a date that would satisfy so many participants was a challenge. The proposed December date Bagley had in mind for the first dinner, although agreed to by the cardinals, had to be changed. The plan was to have entertainment provided by the orchestra and choral group from the Catholic University Benjamin T. Rome School of Music. This would provide an enjoyable evening of music at no additional

The chairman of the First American Cardinals Dinner, Smith Bagley, and his wife, Elizabeth, entering the ballroom.

cost and give the music school students valuable exposure to an influential audience. Bagley arranged a meeting with the dean of the music school, Elaine Walter, to confirm the arrangements only to learn that she had scheduled another engagement for the orchestra and chorus on that precise day.

Ever ready to run right through such obstacles, Bagley arranged for the date of December 12 at the Pension Building, confirmed this with Father Byron, who had Cardinal Hickey and all of the cardinals sign on. The date, site, and participation of cardinals were set. Now all the Board of Regents had to do was fill the hall with 1,000 people paying $1,000 each, enabling Catholic University to reach its goal of grossing $1 million for the university.

Bagley and his fellow regents had an advantage in selling tickets, even at such a high price, because this specific dinner in December 1989 marked the following three events in the history of The Catholic University of America and the national Church.

- The conclusion of the Catholic University centennial celebration.

- The 100th anniversary of the arrival of the first students at Catholic University in the fall of 1889.

- The 200th anniversary of the establishment of the hierarchy of the Church in the United States in the fall of 1789.

Bagley and other regents knew that the secret to filling the hall was to concentrate on selling multiple tables of 10, rather than individual tickets. It was generally understood that each regent would take one table. As the meetings of the Board of Regents progressed, members began committing to selling multiple tables. Week by week, as the table commitments grew and then began to snowball, an atmosphere of success was created and the "buzz" around Washington was that Catholic University was organizing an event of some significance that could become something that everyone should attend.

An indication of how prescient Bagley was is the fact that the American Cardinals Dinner endured for a quarter century in essentially the same form.

The First American Cardinals Dinner, Washington, D.C.

December 12, 1989

A Blueprint for the Future

This first American Cardinals Dinner was a resounding success, with more than 1,300 tickets sold and thousands of dollars coming in from people who could not attend but wanted to support the event and the university.

For the first time in history, all five resident United States cardinals appeared as a group in support of one cause: The Catholic University of America. The five cardinals were cohost Cardinal James Hickey, archbishop of Washington; Cardinal Joseph Bernardin, archbishop of Chicago; Cardinal Bernard Law, archbishop of Boston; Cardinal John O'Connor, archbishop of New York; and Cardinal Edmund Szoka, archbishop of Detroit. Also honored and attending was retired archbishop

of Philadelphia, Cardinal John Krol. Archbishop Pio Laghi, Vatican nuncio the United States, was present as well as Catholic University president and cohost of the event, Rev. William J. Byron, S.J.

Smith Bagley, dinner chairman and founder, along with his wife, Elizabeth, were roundly praised for engineering a huge social and financial success. The hall was filled, although the winter weather did not accommodate as the 1,300 guests arrived in a heavy snowstorm. The dinner raised almost $1.4 million for Catholic University's scholarship programs.

Concelebrating a Mass earlier at the National Shrine of the Immaculate Conception were cardinals Hickey, Bernardin, Law, O'Connor, Szoka, and Krol, as well as Archbishop Laghi and Monsignor Michael J. Bransfield, executive director of the Shrine.

The principal speaker at the dinner was the president of the United States, George H.W. Bush. In his talk he referred to the recent meeting between Pope John Paul II and Soviet leader Mikhail Gorbachev and Gorbachev's newly expressed respect for the value of religious belief. Bush attended the centennial kickoff dinner on April 10, 1987, as vice president and the final centennial event on December 12, 1989, as president.

Entertainment was provided by Catholic University's Symphony Orchestra and University Chorus and Ensembles. Soloists were School of Music alumni Myra Merritt, a Metropolitan Opera principal; and John Aler, a two-time Grammy Award winner and international opera and concert artist; accompanied on piano by Michael Cordovana, conductor of the University Chorus.

The American Cardinals Encouragement Award was created for this dinner with the goal of identifying and encouraging exemplary work in the tradition of Christian service. The award, which consisted of a citation and a $10,000 contribution to the honored effort, recognizes a person and a work committed to Gospel values in the Catholic tradition of providing human service for the love of God. Not eligible were members of the hierarchy, political figures, current Catholic University

The First American Cardinals Dinner, December 12, 1989
Left to right: Cardinal O'Connor, Cardinal Law, Cardinal Hickey, Father Byron, retired archbishop of Philadelphia Cardinal Krol, Cardinal Bernardin, Cardinal Szoka, and Smith Bagley.

Mass in the Crypt Church, National Shrine of the Immaculate Conception, December 12, 1989
Left to right, seated: Cardinal Law, Cardinal Bernardin, Cardinal Hickey, Cardinal Krol, Cardinal O'Connor, and Cardinal Szoka. Standing: Monsignor William A. Kerr, unidentified bishop, Bishop Anthony M. Pilla, Archbishop Anthony J. Bevilacqua, Archbishop William H. Keeler, Monsignor Michael J. Bransfield, Father Byron, Archbishop Eugene A. Marino, Bishop Adam Maida, an unidentified bishop, Bishop John J. Myers, and Rev. Garry Giroux.

The schedule for the cardinals dinner begins with a Mass concelebrated by all the cardinals in the afternoon preceding the event. The first such Mass took place in the Crypt Church of the National Shrine of the Immaculate Conception in Washington, D.C., on the afternoon of The First American Cardinals Dinner.

The Great Hall of the Pension Building. Now known as the National Building Museum, the old Pension Building is a marvel of engineering. Built in the 1880s, it was designed for two distinct functions: as the headquarters for the U.S. Pension Bureau and to provide a suitably grand space for Washington's social and political functions. Its interior is dominated by the Great Hall, a grand central space and the site of The First American Cardinals Dinner in 1989 and the fifth in 1994. These dinners were elegant events, similar to others held over the years, including the 1885 Inaugural Ball of President Grover Cleveland, who, incidentally, attended the groundbreaking ceremony for Caldwell Hall with Cardinal James Gibbons of Baltimore in 1888. Saved from demolition after years of neglect, the historic building was beautifully renovated and restored. The Pension Building is listed on the National Register of Historic Places and in 1997 officially renamed the National Building Museum. The photo above of The First American Cardinals Dinner is by the renowned photographer and Catholic University alumnus Fred J. Maroon, B.Arch. 1950.

trustees, or members of the Catholic University Board of Regents.

Helen Marino Connolly, a Boston-area nurse, received the award for her outstanding work helping and reassuring dying persons and their families as president and executive director of the Good Samaritan Hospice, Brighton, Mass.

In presenting the award to Connolly, Catholic University also saluted all of the nation's hospice programs for providing compassionate, dignified, humane, and loving care for those suffering from terminal illnesses.

The Second American Cardinals Dinner, New York City
January 18, 1991

Following the resounding success of the first dinner in Washington, D.C., cardinals O'Connor, Bernardin, Law, and Szoka signed on to have similar events in their archdioceses. The tentative order was to have the events in New York City, Chicago, Boston, then Detroit. Despite Detroit's Cardinal Edmund Szoka enthusiastic support of Catholic University and of these events,

however, in April 1990 he was transferred to the Vatican curia as president of the Prefecture of the Economic Affairs of the Holy See, placing Detroit on the back burner until it again had a cardinal. In 1991 New York, Washington, Chicago, and Boston were the only United States archdioceses headed by cardinals.

Early in 1990, Cardinal O'Connor agreed to cohost the second dinner. The "cohosting" part of the agreement was important, for he wanted to be certain Catholic University continued to be very active in selling tables and individual tickets at $1,000 each to those associated with the university nationwide to help to fill the Waldorf Astoria Hotel with paying guests.

With the myriad of December activities already scheduled in New York City, Cardinal O'Connor selected the date of January 18, 1991, which the other cardinals and Father Byron found satisfactory. Although this differed with the original Smith Bagley belief that a December date was best because many of the prospective contributors would prefer that month for "end-of-the-year tax purposes," Bagley came to see that it would be even better than the December date.

The Second American Cardinals Dinner
Left to right: Cardinal O'Connor, Father Byron, dinner chairman William E. Simon, Cardinal Hickey, Cardinal Bernardin, and Cardinal Law.

Right: Archbishop Agostino Cacciavillan, apostolic nuncio, with cardinals Bernardin and O'Connor at The Second American Cardinals Dinner in New York.

He realized that since virtually all contributions would be committed by the end of December, with the event itself in January, the donor could choose, for tax purposes, to have his gift recorded in either calendar year. With Cardinal Bernardin agreeing with O'Connor that he, too, would find a December dinner for Catholic University difficult to schedule, Bagley and the Board of Regents now planned to have the dinners each January. Bernardin asked that January 11, 1992, be placed on the calendars of the archbishops of Washington, Boston, New York City, and Detroit.

Attending the second American Cardinals Dinner at the Waldorf Astoria Hotel — once again a resounding success — were all four resident cardinals, cohost Cardinal John O'Connor, Cardinal Joseph Bernardin, Cardinal Bernard Law, and Cardinal James Hickey. Chairman of the event, which was attended by more than 1,000 guests, was former United States Secretary of the Treasury William E. Simon. Three future cardinals were also there: Bishop Edward M. Egan of Bridgeport, Archbishop William H. Keeler of Baltimore, and Archbishop Adam J. Maida of Detroit.

Others present included the Vatican nuncio to the United States, Archbishop Agostino Cacciavillan; Perez de Cuellar, secretary general of the United Nations; Archbishop Renato Martino, nuncio and permanent observer of the Holy See to the United Nations; Richard Thornburgh, attorney general of the United States, and his wife; South Dakota Senator Larry Pressler; and the United States ambassador to the United Nations, Thomas Pickering.

The Second American Cardinals Encouragement Award was presented to Sister Mary Rose McGeady, D.C., president and CEO of Covenant House, New York City.

All of the cardinals concelebrated a Mass prior to the dinner at Saint Patrick's Cathedral. Entertainment was provided by CUA's Benjamin T. Rome School of Music, featuring the piano duo of Elaine Walter and Michael Cordovana, with Jenifer Mason on flute and Maria Goltz on cello. Also delighting the audience was The Catholic University Trio, comprising James Litzelman on piano, Howayda Samandari playing violin, and Li Jie on cello.

The Catholic University Symphony Orchestra with members of the University Chorus provided dinner music as well as presenting selections of Viennese favorites, with solos by Detra Battle, Class of 1989, a 1991 semifinalist at the Metropolitan Opera auditions.

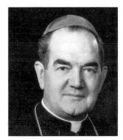

Bishop William J. McDonald M.A. 1937, Rector, 1957–1967

Bishop William J. McDonald, Ninth Rector, Dies at Age 84

Bishop McDonald, rector of The Catholic University of America from 1957 to 1967, died in San Francisco at the age of 84 on January 7, 1989. A native of Ireland, he was ordained in San Francisco in 1928. He served as a parish priest until 1936 when he began his career at The Catholic University of America where he earned master's and doctoral degrees in philosophy. In 1940 he became an instructor in the Catholic University School of Philosophy. He was named an assistant professor in 1944, a full professor in 1950, and vice rector in 1954.

He succeeded Bishop Bryan J. McEntegart as rector in 1957. McDonald's time as rector was characterized by a massive increase in the numbers of undergraduate students and the construction of many buildings. He was appointed auxiliary bishop of Washington in 1964. His rectorship ended in 1967 amid the turmoil of the national campus unrest of the 1960s. Following his tenure as Catholic University rector, he was appointed auxiliary bishop of San Francisco, retiring in 1979. Bishop McDonald was awarded the President's Centennial Medal in 1988 by Rev. William J. Byron, S.J., Catholic University president. In 1989 one of the student residential units of Centennial Village was dedicated McDonald House in honor of Catholic University's ninth rector.

Raymond A. DuFour, B.A. 1928, J.D. 1936, Dies at Age 83

Raymond A. DuFour
B.A. 1928, J.D. 1936

A lifelong Catholic University enthusiast, Ray DuFour, for whom the Raymond A. DuFour Athletic Center is named, passed away in Delray, Fla., on September 15, 1990. He entered Catholic University in 1924 on a football scholarship, earned undergraduate and law degrees, and became involved with the university for the remainder of his life as an active alumnus, trustee, and generous benefactor. In addition to his key involvement in developing a complete athletic complex on North Campus, he was a major benefactor of the Columbus School of Law building. The name Raymond A. DuFour is indelibly inscribed in the ledger of principal Catholic University alumni and benefactors.

Consistory of June 1991 (Mahony, Bevilacqua)

Pope John Paul II created 22 new cardinals on June 28 1991, including two from the United States, Catholic University alumnus Roger M. Mahony of Los Angeles and Anthony J. Bevilacqua of Philadelphia.

Cardinal Roger Mahony
Archbishop of Los Angeles
M.S.W. 1964

Cardinal Anthony Bevilacqua
Archbishop of Philadelphia

Cardinal John Krol with Pope John Paul II, taken at the Vatican, during the Catholic University centennial celebrations. Cardinal Krol, moderator of the Catholic University Board of Regents, convened the centennial board meeting of the regents at the Vatican. The First American Cardinals Dinner was the concluding event of the Catholic University centennial.

The Third American Cardinals Dinner, Chicago

January 11, 1992

This was the last American Cardinals Dinner for Father William J. Byron, S.J. In the spring of 1991, Father Byron announced he was stepping down in June 1992, his 65th birthday, after 10 years as president of Catholic University, making the Windy City gala a well deserved send-off to a beloved leader who accomplished great things for the university.

Cardinal Bernardin cohosted the dinner at the Chicago Hilton and Towers following a Mass in Holy Name Cathedral. Five of the six resident cardinals attended, including Roger Mahony, Los Angeles; Bernard Law, Boston; James Hickey, Washington; Anthony Bevilacqua, Philadelphia; and Bernardin. Cardinal O'Connor was unable to attend as he was suffering from the flu, contracted during a meeting with Itzak Shamir in Israel.

This was the first dinner for cardinals Mahony and Bevilacqua, who had received red hats from Pope John Paul II seven months earlier. Also attending was Cardinal Pio Laghi, prefect of the Congregation for Catholic Education. He was Vatican nuncio to the United States from 1980 to 1990 and attended the first cardinals dinner in that position. Laghi's successor as nuncio, Archbishop Agostino Cacciavillan, also attended this event.

Chairman of the Chicago dinner was Michael R. Quinlan, who had a storybook rise to CEO and chairman of the board of McDonald's Corporation of Oak Brook, Ill. He started at McDonald's in 1963 as a part-time mailroom employee, working through the ranks to become president and chief operating officer in 1982, chief executive officer in 1987, and chairman in 1990. Vice chairman of the dinner and chairman of the Catholic University Board of Regents was Timothy J. May, Esq. Chicago Mayor Richard Daly delivered welcoming remarks to the more than 900 guests.

Principal speaker Francesco Cossiga, president of Italy, was presented with an honorary degree. He praised American Catholics "for influencing the universal Church in its mission of salvation and for promoting human values worldwide."

Receiving the Third Annual American Cardinal's

The Third American Cardinals Dinner
Left to right: Monsignor William A. Kerr, Catholic University vice president for university relations; Cardinal Mahony; Cardinal Law; Vincent P. Walter Jr., vice president and general secretary of the university; Cardinal Bernardin; Father Byron; Cardinal Hickey; and Cardinal Bevilacqua.

McMahon Hall

During Father Byron's tenure, this historic building, constructed in 1895, underwent extensive renovations and restoration. Originally called McMahon Hall of Philosophy, it was named for Monsignor James McMahon, a New York pastor who contributed real estate valued at $400,000, which was used for its construction. In its foyer is a heroic-size marble statue of Pope Leo XIII, who authorized the founding of Catholic University in 1887.

Encouragement Award was Suzy Yehl Marta, of Palatine, Ill., founder of the Rainbows For All God's Children, a program that helped children cope with divorce and death. "The myth that kids bounce back from divorce and death persists," she said. "They can't grieve effectively and many turn to drugs and alcohol."

The background music and dinner entertainment was provided by the Catholic University Symphony Orchestra, conducted by Randall Craig Fleischer, and the Catholic University Concert Chorus, featuring soloists Lara Colby, Jamet Pittman, and Mark Forrest. They received two standing ovations during their performances.

Caldwell Hall

Catholic University's historic first building. Ground was broken and the cornerstone laid in 1888. It was formally dedicated and opened November 13, 1889. Originally named Divinity Hall, it was soon called Caldwell Hall in recognition of Mary Gwendoline Caldwell, who contributed $300,000 for the building's construction. She was a young 21-year-old heiress to a fortune made in gas companies and Kentucky real estate. It has a chapel where daily Mass is said. An addition, known as the Seton Wing, was built in 1960. The Caldwell Hall interior has been renovated and updated several times.

Father Byron Ends His Tenure, July 1992

One of Father Byron's final events as president, on May 23, 1992, was the groundbreaking for the new Columbus School of Law building and the accompanying lower level garage on the site of the old football field.

A host of other improvements took place during Father Byron's final school year, including the following:

- The continuation of the four-year renovation and restoration program of McMahon Hall to restore the luster and grandeur of this beautiful building dedicated in 1895.

- Enhanced landscaping around Centennial Village.

- Improved dining facilities in the North Dining Hall as well as in Curley and Caldwell halls.

- Renovations to Pangborn Hall.

- Improved facilities in University Center.

- A new roof on Marist Hall.

- Upgrades to computer equipment in Pangborn Hall and a new computer classroom added in McMahon Hall.

- Demolitions included a block of Catholic University-owned buildings on Monroe Street on South Campus. On the main campus, the old stadium press box and what remained of the stadium stands were removed in anticipation of the construction of the new law school building and St. John's Hall and Zimmerman Hall were demolished.

Caldwell Hall Chapel can accommodate about 120 and is the original university chapel.

CHAPTER TWO

Chapter Two

Brother Patrick Ellis, F.S.C.
Catholic University President
1992–1998

Brother Patrick Ellis, F.S.C., succeeds Rev. William J. Byron, S.J.

In late January 1992, two weeks after The Third American Cardinals Dinner, it was announced that a new president had been selected to replace Father Byron. Brother Patrick Ellis, F.S.C., an alumnus of Catholic University, became the 13th president, the second member of a religious community (Father Byron being the first), and the first religious brother. All of the early heads of Catholic University were diocesan priests and were called "rector." Clarence Walton, the 10th leader was the first layman and first to be called "president" rather than "rector." (His successor, Edmund D. Pellegrino, M.D., was the second layman and the current president, John Garvey, the third.)

Born Harry James Ellis Jr. on November 17, 1928, in Baltimore, he took the name of Brother Felician Patrick when he entered the Institute of the Brothers of the Christian Schools, but he was always called Brother Patrick. He began teaching after graduating summa cum laude in 1951 from The Catholic University of America. He received a Ph.D. in English from the University of Pennsylvania in 1960 while also teaching at West Philadelphia Catholic High School for Boys. He distinguished himself as president of La Salle University, Philadelphia, from 1977 to 1992, the longest tenure in the university's history. When Brother Patrick Ellis officially took over at Catholic University on August 1, 1992, he was 64 years old, only one year younger than Father Byron who just retired. He was installed on December 10, 1992.

From the first day of his administration, the enhancement of Catholic University's computer technology was high on Brother Patrick's "must do" list. Over the years he advanced this area with enthusiasm and with constant reminders to his

Brother Patrick Ellis, F.S.C.

staff to keep abreast of the ever-advancing aspects of the computer world. "Think future all the time" was Brother Patrick's continual refrain. He effected the completion of up-to-date fiber-optic wiring for a high-speed computer network. Desiring to share the Catholic University assets, Brother Patrick secured a major grant for Catholic University's computer center and School of Engineering to give 15 Catholic high schools in the Metropolitan Washington area access to the Internet by connecting to the university's computer network.

In another local initiative, the former University College was renamed Metropolitan College and, to provide additional educational opportunities to all in the community, started offering many scholarships to minorities.

This was an ongoing and successful enterprise,

with Catholic University being lauded for the positive impact it was making on the local Washington scene.

In addition, on September 1, 1992, the School of Architecture and Planning was created. It was then and continues to be the Washington area's largest architecture school. Early on, Brother Patrick made provisions for improved lighting in all areas of the campus, oversaw the construction of a new entrance to Pangborn Hall, and enhanced the university's ongoing commitment to maintaining a beautifully landscaped campus. With the many changes to the campus and the ever-evolving needs of the student body, Brother Patrick also began to focus on the urgent need for a new student center, which did not materialize until the tenure of his successor.

Columbus School of Law
The $32 million state-of-the-art Columbus School of Law building.

Columbus School of Law
Dean Ralph Rohner and law school alumna Louise M. Keelty assisted Cardinal Adam Maida and Brother Patrick Ellis, F.S.C. at the dedication ceremony.

The Columbus School of Law of The Catholic University of America

The CUA law school has a long and cherished history. It opened in McMahon Hall in 1877 and moved off campus to 18th Street, N.W., Washington, D.C., in 1954 with its merger with Columbus University Law School. In 1966 the law school returned to campus in newly opened Leahy Hall. Two decades later, with a greatly expanded student body and classes being held in several different buildings, plans were initiated for the construction of a new building, resulting in the October 1999 dedication of the current state-of-the-art facility.

Columbus School of Law
Mary, Mirror of Justice chapel.

The Fourth American Cardinals Dinner, Boston
April 24, 1993

The fourth dinner had its anxious moments before arrangements were finalized. Less than a week after the success of the Chicago dinner, Father Byron, who was stepping down in six months, learned that the next event could not take place as scheduled in January 1993 because the leaders of the annual Boston Catholic Charities gala scheduled for the following month did not want invitations to the Catholic University event going out first to essentially the same group of prospects. Early in 1992, Monsignor William A. Kerr, vice president for university relations and principal "point-man" for the cardinals dinner, shuttled to Boston numerous times to confer with Cardinal Law and his associates, for it was vital to Catholic University that the continuity not be broken and the Boston event be held, regardless of the date. Monsignor Kerr found the atmosphere in the Archdiocese of Boston among both clerical and lay leaders to be less than enthusiastic toward having an event requiring extensive hours of arm-twisting for a project that would not benefit the archdiocese, which itself was going through tough fiscal trials. Cardinal Law, however, did not back down and the event received a new date of April 24, 1993.

It was very important to Father Byron that he leave his successor not only a legacy of successful annual dinners, which were becoming solidly embedded in the calendars of the university and each cardinal, but also a lineup of commitments for the next few years, especially as Monsignor Kerr, the key organizer of the dinners, was also leaving to become president of LaRoche College. As a result, Brother Patrick Ellis took over in August of 1992 with Cardinal Law of Boston committed to a dinner in April 1993, Cardinal Mahony having a January 1994 date on his calendar in Los Angeles, and Cardinal Bevilacqua scheduled for early 1995 in Philadelphia.

The Boston dinner continued the tradition of success, not only financially, but in attendance, with eight cardinals present, the most ever to appear at one time for a charity event. Brother Patrick and cohost Cardinal Law were joined by cardinals Bernardin, Hickey, Mahony, and Bevilacqua.

Three special guests from Rome also attended: Cardinal William Baum, apostolic penitentiary, former archbishop of Washington and former chancellor of Catholic University; Cardinal Edmund Szoka, president of the Prefecture of the Economic Affairs of the Holy See, who was at the first cardinals dinner as archbishop of Detroit; and Cardinal Pio Laghi, prefect of the Congregation for Catholic Education and Vatican nuncio to the United States from 1980 to 1990. Laghi also attended the first cardinals dinner. The current apostolic nuncio, Archbishop Agostino Cacciavillan, also was present. Cardinal O'Connor had to cancel his attendance at the last minute. A Mass was concelebrated before the dinner in the Cathedral of the Holy Cross.

Raymond L. Flynn, mayor of Boston since 1984 and recently named fourth United States ambassador to the Holy See (where he served from 1993 to 1997), welcomed the approximately 1,000 guests. Dinner cochairman, Thomas J. Flatley, founder and president of The Flatley Company, also spoke. Joining as cochair was Thomas A. Vanderslice, chairman and CEO of M/A-Com, Inc., who had earned a Ph.D. from Catholic University in 1956.

The chairman of the Catholic University Board of Regents, Timothy J. May, Esq., addressed the attendees and introduced the regents' chair-elect, R. Kathleen Perini.

The American Cardinals Encouragement Award was presented to Anne Burns, founder-director of the St. John and St. Hugh Family AIDS Project, Dorchester, Mass.

Dinner music and entertainment was provided by student musicians from the Benjamin T. Rome School of Music. Forty-five of the usual 85-member Catholic University Symphony Orchestra and a group from the 150-member chorus performed under the baton of Randall Craig Fleischer.

The Fourth American Cardinals Dinner
Left to right, seated: Cardinal Hickey, Cardinal Szoka, Cardinal Baum, and Cardinal Mahony. Standing: Cardinal Laghi, Brother Patrick, Cardinal Law, and Cardinal Bernardin. Missing from the photo is Cardinal Bevilacqua.

Left to right: Cardinal Bernardin, Cardinal Baum, Brother Patrick, Cardinal Law, Cardinal Mahony, Cardinal Szoka, Cardinal Bevilacqua, and Cardinal Laghi. Missing from the photo is Cardinal Hickey.

The Fifth American Cardinals Dinner, Washington, D.C.
April 16, 1994

At the conclusion of the Boston dinner in April 1993, Cardinal Roger Mahony of Los Angeles stepped to the podium for the closing prayer and to offer remarks about the venue for the next dinner. He stated, "Next year, I have the privilege of serving as host for this magnificent affair in Los Angeles. The date is January 17, 1994, and if your interest in Catholic University isn't sufficient inducement to join us, may I remind you the average daily temperature in L.A. in mid-January is 65 degrees."

The audience roared their approval and the gala ended.

At 4 a.m. on January 17, 1994, a devastating earthquake hit Los Angeles. The Cathedral of Saint Vibiana, where the Mass preceding the dinner was to take place, was among the sites severely affected. The earthquake, measuring 6.6 on the Richter scale, rocked Los Angeles and caused massive destruction, with emergency crews pulling bodies out of collapsed buildings in a frantic effort to save lives. Mayor Richard Riordan of Los Angeles declared a state of emergency, imposed an evening curfew, and begged people to stay home. Ultimately it was calculated that 60 people died, close to 8,000 were injured, and more than 5,000 buildings were deemed unsafe, including the Los Angeles Cathedral of Saint Vibiana.

Fortunately, several months earlier Cardinal Mahony had changed the date of the dinner from January 17 to April 16. However, with the Church providing solace to those affected by the earthquake and tending to those whose lives were in turmoil, a spring dinner was furthermost from his mind. Brother Patrick, Vincent P. Walter, and their associates at Catholic University quickly took charge and moved the dinner to Washington. Notices with the reason explained were sent to all Catholic University constituents. They read: "Same Date, Different City."

The dinner, attended by 800 guests, was the second for Brother Patrick and was held at Pension Hall in the National Building Museum, the site of the first dinner in 1989.

All six resident cardinals attended, including Cardinal Mahony, who was still staggered by the January earthquake in his city and who received extended applause for his heroic efforts in assisting those affected. The others were cohost Cardinal Hickey, Cardinal Bernardin, Cardinal Bevilacqua, Cardinal O'Connor, and Cardinal Law. Also attending was the apostolic nuncio in Washington, D.C., Archbishop Agostino Cacciavillan.

The predinner Mass was held in the Crypt Church of the Basilica of The National Shrine of the Immaculate Conception. Chair of the Catholic University Board of Regents, Kathleen Perini, who, with husband Dominick, owned Perini Construction, served as chair of the dinner. Their son, Paul, was a Catholic University graduate. The Cardinals Encouragement Award was presented to Sister Carol Keehan, D.C., president and chief executive officer of Washington's Providence Hospital.

Brother Gregory Nugent, F.S.C.
CUA Alumnus

Brother Gregory Nugent, F.S.C., Dies June 20, 1992 at Age 80

Brother Gregory Nugent, F.S.C., for whom Nugent Hall was named, died on June 20, 1992, shortly after he retired as special assistant to the president and secretary to the Board of Trustees, a position he held for 12 years under three presidents. A Catholic University alumnus, Brother Gregory was president of Manhattan College, Riverdale, N.Y., from 1962 to 1975. He was a trustee of Catholic University before becoming a key member of the university administration in 1980, under president Edmund D. Pellegrino, M.D. He continued during the entire regime of Father William J. Byron, S. J., and the early days of Brother Patrick Ellis, F.S.C. The executive office building was named Nugent Hall in 1991.

The Fifth American Cardinals Dinner
Left to right: Cardinals Mahony, Bernardin, Hickey, Law, O'Connor, and Bevilacqua, and Brother Patrick.

The early 1990s saw an addition to the St. Vincent de Paul Chapel, pictured here, which was constructed between Ryan Hall and Regan Hall, in 1949.

George J. Quinn
B.C.E. 1950

George J. Quinn, B.C.E. 1950, Dies at Age 80

George J. Quinn, alumnus and trustee, was a generous supporter of the American Cardinals Dinner from the first event until his death on August 16, 1994. The Catholic University Alumni Association honored him with the Cardinal Gibbons Medal in 1992. He established the Quinn Family Trust to help Catholic University students needing financial aid. He also initiated Engineering 2000, an annual summer program that provided scholarships for more than 100 high school students to come to Catholic University to learn about engineering education and careers. He was survived by his wife, Eileen S. Quinn. In 1989 one of the student residential units of Centennial Village was dedicated Quinn House in honor of this illustrious Catholic University alumnus.

Benjamin T. Rome
M.Arch. 1934

Benjamin T. Rome, M.Arch. 1934, Dies at Age 88

Benjamin T. Rome was a generous donor, dedicated to his alma mater. He was born to Jewish parents in Baltimore. His father's friendship with Cardinal James Gibbons, archbishop of Baltimore, began Rome's lifelong ties with the Catholic Church. In the mid-1920s, he moved to Washington, D.C., to work for the George Hyman Construction Company, which he eventually led as chairman. After being refused admission by other universities, Rome was accepted by Catholic University as a graduate student in architecture, earning his M.Arch. in 1934. He was a music lover and began funding annual concerts by the Catholic University School of Music at the John F. Kennedy Center for the Performing Arts, a practice he continued year after year. The music school was renamed for him. Private and reserved, Rome expanded his philanthropy to the music school and other Catholic University projects. He was named to the Catholic University Board of Trustees, and received the Cardinal Gibbons Medal in 1971 and an honorary degree when he became trustee emeritus after serving on the board for 12 years. He also was named a Knight Commander of the Order of St. Sylvester, the highest honor the Vatican can bestow on a non-Catholic. He died on June 10, 1994.

Consistory of November 1994 (Keeler, Maida)

A consistory was held by Pope John Paul II on November 26, 1994, naming 30 cardinals, including William H. Keeler of Baltimore and Adam J. Maida of Detroit. At that point, there were 12 living United States cardinals. By the end of 1996, there were two fewer: John J. Krol of Philadelphia died in March and Joseph L. Bernardin of Chicago in November.

Cardinal William Keeler
Archbishop of Baltimore

Cardinal Adam Maida
Archbishop of Detroit

A view of the Basilica of the National Shrine of the Immaculate Conception from the campus.

The Sixth American Cardinals Dinner, Philadelphia
February 25, 1995

After holding the prior two American Cardinals Dinners in the spring, the sixth dinner in Philadelphia, which was on the calendar of Cardinal Anthony Bevilacqua for almost three years, reverted to the "early in the year" tradition with the cardinal cohosting the event with Brother Patrick in late February 1995.

At this point there were two additional resident United States cardinals, William H. Keeler of Baltimore and Adam J. Maida of Detroit.

All eight cardinal archbishops in the United States attended: Cardinal Bernardin, Cardinal Law, Cardinal O'Connor, Cardinal Hickey, Cardinal Mahony, Cardinal Bevilacqua, Cardinal Keeler, and Cardinal Maida. A ninth cardinal, the retired archbishop of Philadelphia, Cardinal John Krol, was also present. Having nine resident cardinals attend this dinner was a great achievement for Catholic University. Except for the gathering of

all bishops at the annual Bishop's Conference in Washington each fall, this was the first time nine United States cardinals, including all eight active ordinaries, gathered for one specific cause—in this case Catholic University. That these cardinals arranged their busy schedules to all be present is a tribute to them as well as an indication of the importance of Catholic University to the Church in America.

Cardinal Bevilacqua was celebrant and homilist at the predinner Mass at Philadelphia's Cathedral Basilica of Saints Peter and Paul. Concelebrating were Cardinal Krol, as well as all the other cardinals. This was to be the last cardinals dinner and Mass for Cardinal Krol, who passed away at 85 years of age on March 3, 1996.

The cochairs of the dinner, which was held at the Pennsylvania Convention Center in Philadelphia, were Joseph F. Paquette Jr., of the PECO Energy Company, and Leonard Abramson, of US Healthcare. Pennsylvania Governor Thomas Ridge delivered a greeting to the 1,500 dinner guests. Former Governor Robert Casey Sr. was also in attendance. Sister Eileen Smith, S.S.J., accepted

The Sixth American Cardinals Dinner
Left to right: Cardinals Keeler, Law, and Bevilacqua; Brother Patrick; and cardinals Hickey, Mahony, and Maida. Missing from photo are cardinals Bernardin, O'Connor, and Krol.

A view of the Edward J. Pryzbyla University Center lawn.

the Cardinals Encouragement Award for St. Vincent's Dining Room of Philadelphia, a soup kitchen, health center, and legal clinic for the poor. In attendance were two future cardinals, Bishop Donald W. Wuerl of Pittsburgh, who became a cardinal in 2010 as archbishop of Washington, and the former rector of North American College in Rome, Monsignor Edwin F. O'Brien, who became archbishop of Baltimore and later was named a cardinal as Grand Master of the Order of the Holy Sepulchre. Former Catholic University president Clarence C. Walton attended, as did both United States senators from Pennsylvania, Arlen Specter and Robert Casey Jr., as well as the apostolic nuncio, Archbishop Agostino Cacciavillan.

Commencement Exercises take place in May on the University Mall adjacent to the Basilica of the National Shrine of the Immaculate Conception.

The Seventh American Cardinals Dinner, Los Angeles
April 19, 1996

The first American Cardinals Dinner held on the West Coast and the seventh overall was cohosted by Cardinal Roger Mahony, archbishop of Los Angeles, and Brother Patrick Ellis, F.S.C., at the Regent Beverly Wilshire, Beverly Hills, Calif.

The dinner honored the eight cardinals resident in United States, all of whom attended. In addition, the apostolic nuncio, Archbishop Agostino Cacciavillan, was there. Showing his support for Catholic University, Cardinal O'Connor flew to Los Angeles for the dinner and immediately after caught a "red eye" flight to attend "an immovable meeting" in New York.

The cardinals concelebrated the predinner Mass at the Church of the Good Shepherd, Beverly Hills, rather than the usual local cathedral, St. Vibiana, the Los Angeles cathedral for more than a century, which was still closed due to structural damage caused by the 1994 earthquake.

This was to be the last American Cardinals

Dinner for Cardinal Bernardin, who had a sudden recurrence of cancer and passed away in November at age 68. He had attended each cardinals dinner since the beginning.

Alluding to the national scope and impact that Catholic University has been providing to the Church in all parts of the nation, Cardinal Mahony said, "More than 500 priests, nuns, and brothers from California are alumni of Catholic University. The proceeds of the seventh dinner, totaling $1 million, will provide financial aid to West Coast students planning to attend Catholic University."

Chairman of the dinner was John F. Watkins of Pasadena and an all-star committee of 26 prominent Californians. Los Angeles Mayor Richard Riordan welcomed the guests. Patrick Carfizzi, Benjamin T. Rome School of Music class of 1996, sang the National Anthem. The Catholic University Singers, directed by Michael Cordovana and Maureen Codelka, provided the music, with the finale by Mark Forrest, Class of 1995.

The Cardinals Encouragement Award was presented to Richard Bautista, a 13-year-old Whittier shooting victim who asked the people of Los Angeles to pray for his attackers.

The Seventh American Cardinals Dinner
Left to right, seated: Cardinals Bernardin, Mahony, Hickey, and Law. Standing: Cardinals Keeler and O'Connor, Brother Patrick, Cardinals Maida and Bevilacqua.

Among the special guests at the Los Angeles dinner were Bob and Dolores Hope, here flanking Cardinal Bernardin.

Among the special guests at the Los Angeles dinner were Bob and Dolores Hope. Bob was a few weeks shy of his 93rd birthday. Seated with them was Monsignor Michael J. Bransfield, rector of the Basilica of the National Shrine of the Immaculate Conception. The Hopes funded a chapel in the Basilica. Dolores, a lifelong Catholic, witnessed the conversion of Bob to Catholicism before he died. Both Dolores and Bob lived to be 102. In an interview Hope's grandson, Zach Hope, said that when asked on his deathbed where he wanted to be buried, a comedian to the end, Hope replied,

"Surprise me." Bob and Dolores are interred in the Bob Hope Memorial Garden at San Fernando Mission Cemetery in Los Angeles, where his mother is also buried.

Cardinal John Krol
Archbishop of Philadelphia
J.C.D. 1942

Cardinal John Krol Dies at Age 85

At his death on March 3, 1996, John J. Krol, retired archbishop of Philadelphia, had been a priest for 59 years, a bishop for 42 years, and a cardinal for 28 years. Krol attended The First American Cardinals Dinner in Washington in December 1989 and the sixth in Philadelphia in 1995.

Cardinal Joseph Bernardin
Archbishop of Chicago
M.A. 1951

Cardinal Joseph Bernardin Dies at Age 68

Joseph L. Bernardin was in complete agreement that the cardinals dinners should be a "must" function for each cardinal to attend each year unless an extraordinary occurrence kept them away. He attended each of the seven dinners from the first until he passed away on November 14, 1996. He hosted the third dinner in Chicago in 1992. He announced in late August 1996 that a previously diagnosed cancer had suddenly re-appeared and he died 11 weeks later. He was 68 and had been a priest for 44 years, bishop for 30 years, and cardinal for 14 years.

Gibbons Hall

The Eighth American Cardinals Dinner, Detroit

June 6, 1997

The Eighth American Cardinals Dinner was held at the Ritz-Carlton Hotel in Dearborn, Mich. Brother Patrick cohosted the event with Detroit's Cardinal Maida, who was in Poland until the night before the dinner, attending the 46th International Eucharistic Congress in Wroclaw. Honored at the dinner were cardinals Hickey, Law, Mahony, Keeler, and Maida. With 125 tables sold, the Detroit dinner raised $1.25 million.

Cardinal Maida was the principal celebrant at the predinner Mass at Blessed Sacrament Cathedral in Detroit.

The Cardinal's Encouragement Award was presented to Angels' Place, an Oakland County, Mich., organization founded in 1992 that provides homes to developmentally disabled adults whose parents or guardians can no longer care for them. Angels' Place cofounder Loretta Nagle said, "Many of the residents' families have exhausted their physical and emotional strength, as well as their financial resources." Cardinal Maida commented, "Angels' Place provides residents with a warm, Christian atmosphere in which they receive love, respect, and an opportunity to develop personally and spiritually."

Dinner cochairs were Michael Monahan, president of Comerica Bank, and Monsignor Ricardo Bass, pastor of St. Joan of Arc Parish, St. Clair Shores, Mich., who had earned a canon law degree at Catholic University and was a past president of the Canon Law Society of America.

Shortly after this dinner, Brother Patrick announced he would step down the following year after six years as Catholic University president.

The Eighth American Cardinals Dinner
Left to right, seated: Cardinals Law, Maida, and Hickey. Standing: Cardinal Mahony, Brother Patrick, and Cardinal Keeler.

The Ninth American Cardinals Dinner, Baltimore

May 1, 1998

The ninth dinner was held in Baltimore, the first time for that city. The $1,000-a-plate, black-tie dinner, which each year had attracted prominent Catholics from across the country, was cohosted by Baltimore's Cardinal Keeler and held at the Baltimore Convention Center. It was the last of six American Cardinals dinners cohosted by Brother Patrick, who had announced he would be stepping down as president. Brother Patrick commented that he felt he was coming home: he was born in Baltimore and attended high school there at Calvert Hall, which was taught by the Brothers of the Christian Schools and where he found his vocation to enter their congregation. Shortly before this dinner, it was announced that Brother Patrick would be succeeded as president by Rev. David M. O'Connell, C.M.

Honored at the gala were six of the eight cardinals who serve in United States archdioceses: Washington's James A. Hickey, Boston's Bernard F. Law, Philadelphia's Anthony J. Bevilacqua, Los Angeles's Roger M. Mahony, Detroit's Adam J. Maida, and Baltimore's Keeler. Prior to the dinner all six concelebrated a Mass in the Basilica of the National Shrine of the Assumption of the Blessed Virgin Mary, the first cathedral in the United States.

Cardinal O'Connor of New York planned to attend but became ill and cancelled at the last moment. Chicago's Francis E. George, who had become a cardinal three months earlier, had an engagement planned before his elevation. Richard O. Berndt, managing partner of a local law firm, and Michael J. Batza Jr., chairman and CEO of Heritage Properties, were cochairs of the event. Approximately 1,200 people attended the dinner, which raised more than $1.4 million for Catholic University scholarships.

The Ninth American Cardinals Dinner
Left to right, seated: Cardinals Mahony, Law, Keeler, and Hickey. Standing: Cardinal Maida, Brother Patrick, and Cardinal Bevilacqua.

The Cardinals Encouragement Award went to the oldest Catholic elementary school in Baltimore, the 150-year-old Saints James and John school, where the majority of students were from low-income families. The principal for 17 years, LaUanah King-Cassell, accepted the $10,000 cash prize that accompanied the award, saying, "Saints James and John has been a beacon of hope for the people of East Baltimore. The Christian values we give to our students make all the difference in the world in their learning. The children come to our school and learn how to respect others, how to handle conflict and how to respect authority." She said, "We were working on a technology plan for the school and had acquired a few computers with grocery receipts. This award will allow us to get more than two dozen new computers."

At a press conference earlier in the day, Cardinal Keeler spoke of the relationship of Baltimore with Catholic University and recalled Baltimore's key role in the university's founding. "At the Third Plenary Council of Baltimore in 1884, Archbishop James Gibbons presided, and he was directed to form a committee which would consider the establishment of what in time became the Catholic University. The bishops of the United States met here in 1889 to commemorate the 100th anniversary of the formal establishing of the Catholic Church, and at the time of their meeting went to Washington for the formal inauguration of the new university.

"From that date until his death in 1921, Cardinal Gibbons was the university's chancellor and took a very active part in board meetings and other events relating to its early development. For this reason, it's really appropriate that we do our bit to continue to support it," he said.

The 1998 dinner in Baltimore completed the cycle of having an American Cardinals Dinner in each city led by a resident United States cardinal. Eight different cities had had at least one cardinals dinner to benefit The Catholic University of America scholarship fund: Washington, D.C., (which had two), New York City, Chicago, Boston, Philadelphia, Los Angeles, Detroit, and Baltimore.

Consistory of February 1998 (Stafford, George)

At the last consistory of the millennium on February 21, 1998, Pope John Paul II appointed 22 new cardinals, including two Americans, both Catholic University alumni: J. Francis Stafford in the curia and Francis E. George of Chicago.

At this point, active cardinals were in eight sees: New York (O'Connor), Washington (Hickey), Philadelphia (Bevilacqua), Detroit (Maida), Baltimore (Keeler), Boston (Law), Los Angeles (Mahony), and Chicago (George). There were three cardinals in the curia: Baum, Szoka, and Stafford, and one retired cardinal, John J. Carberry of St. Louis. This is a total of 12 United States cardinals, all except Carberry under 80.

Cardinal J. Francis Stafford
Vatican Curia
M.S.W. 1964

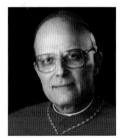

Cardinal Francis George
Archbishop of Chicago
M.A. 1964

—

CHAPTER THREE

Chapter Three

Very Rev. David M. O'Connell, C.M.
Catholic University President
1998–2010

 ev. David M. O'Connell, C.M. succeeds Brother Patrick Ellis, F.S.C.

Father David M. O'Connell, C.M., was named the 14th president of The Catholic University of America in 1998. A double alumnus, he became the third consecutive member of a religious congregation to lead the university.

Father O'Connell was born April 21, 1955, in Philadelphia. After studies at St. Joseph Preparatory High School, Princeton, he continued his education at Niagara University, where he obtained a bachelor's degree in philosophy in 1978. He prepared for the priesthood in Mary Immaculate Seminary, Northampton, Pa., where he received a master of divinity degree in 1981 and a master's degree in moral theology in 1983.

On May 29, 1982, he was ordained a priest of the Eastern Province of the Congregation of the Mission, popularly known as the Vincentians. Following ordination, Father O'Connell's first assignment was at Archbishop Wood High School, Warminster, Pa., where he served from 1982 to 1985.

He continued his studies at The Catholic University of America, earning a licentiate in canon law in 1987, followed by a doctorate in canon law in 1990, after which he joined St. John's University, New York. He served as academic dean there for the following eight years, until he was named president of The Catholic University of America.

Among the many highlights of his presidency was serving as a member of the planning committee for Pope Benedict XVI's 2008 pastoral visit to the United States and hosting the Holy Father on April 17, 2008, at Catholic University. The Pope delivered an address to Catholic educators in the Edward J. Pryzbyla University Center on Catholic University's campus.

Very Rev. David M. O'Connell, C.M.

Left to right: Cardinal Keeler and Cardinal Law, Father O'Connell, Cardinal Hickey, Cardinal Bevilacqua, Cardinal George, and Cardinal Maida at the Mass inaugurating Very Rev. David M. O'Connell, C.M., as 14th president of The Catholic University of America, in the Basilica of the National Shrine of the Immaculate Conception.

Father O'Connell and CUA chancellor Cardinal James Hickey at the inauguration.

Very Reverend David M. O'Connell, C.M., at his inauguration as 14th president of The Catholic University of America.

Benjamin T. Rome School of Music

Entertainment at each of the cardinals dinners has been expertly provided by students, alumni, and faculty of the Benjamin T. Rome School of Music.

Considered the preeminent Catholic center for music study and performance in the United States, The Catholic University of America has long been committed to educating musicians, scholars, and composers. In the 1920s, the university began offering music courses off campus. The music department moved onto the campus in 1950, becoming the School of Music in 1965. It was renamed the Benjamin T. Rome School of Music in 1984, in honor of alumnus, trustee emeritus, and longtime friend and benefactor, the late Benjamin T. Rome. Dean John Paul and his successors, Thomas Mastroianni, Elaine R. Walter, Marilyn Neeley, Murry Sidlin, and Grayson Wagstaff, have shaped a school where performance and scholarship receive equal attention to benefit undergraduate and graduate students who come from across the globe. The school is accredited by the National Association of Schools of Music and is Washington, D.C.'s only university school of music.

The school offers approximately 35 degree

Entrance to Ward Hall, home of the music school.

programs, including Bachelor of Music, Bachelor of Arts in Music, Master of Arts, Master of Music, Master of Music in Sacred Music, Doctor of Musical Arts, Doctor of Musical Arts in Sacred Music, and Doctor of Philosophy in Musicology. Students have the opportunity to work with an impressive faculty of artists and scholars and participate in master classes offered by some of the world's most respected performers. The school also maintains a three-decade-long emphasis on Latin American culture through its Latin American Center for Graduate Studies in Music, which was one of the first of its kind in the nation, as well as the Institute of Sacred Music and the international Center for Ward Method Studies in Gregorian chant. More than 2,000 Catholic University music alumni currently maintain high professional visibility on six continents as performers, music educators, composers, liturgical musicians, and scholars. The Benjamin T. Rome School of Music is recognized for perpetuating the Catholic

Church's historical role in uplifting the human spirit through the study and performance of music.

The 10th American Cardinals Dinner, Boston
April 23, 1999

The cohosts of The 10th American Cardinals Dinner were the new president of The Catholic University of America, Very Rev. David M. O'Connell, C.M., along with the archbishop of Boston and chairman of the Catholic University Board of Trustees, Cardinal Bernard Law. The reception was held at the Commonwealth Pier and the dinner at the World Trade Center, Boston.

Seven cardinals were in attendance, including six who were resident in the United States: Cardinal Hickey, Cardinal Mahony, Cardinal Bevilacqua, Cardinal Keeler, Cardinal Maida, and Cardinal Law. The seventh was Cardinal Pio Laghi, no

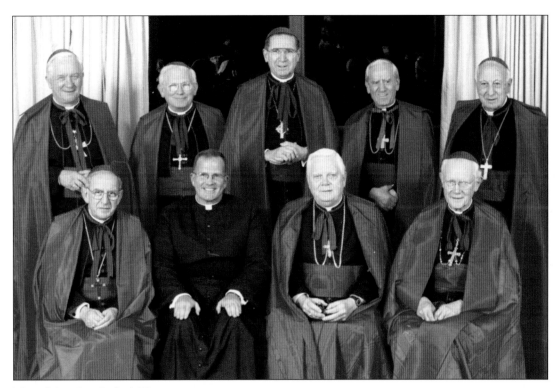

The 10th American Cardinals Dinner
Left to right, seated: Archbishop Gabriel Montalvo, Father O'Connell, and Cardinals Law and Hickey.
Standing: Cardinals Maida, Keeler, Mahony, Bevilacqua, and Laghi.

stranger to the American scene, who represented the Holy See in the United States from 1980 to 1990, and attended The First American Cardinals Dinner. At the time of the 10th dinner, Laghi was in the Vatican curia. The other two resident cardinals, Cardinal George and Cardinal O'Connor, were unable to attend. The cardinals concelebrated a Mass before the dinner at Boston's Cathedral of the Holy Cross. Attending his first American Cardinals Dinner was the new apostolic nuncio, Archbishop Gabriel Montalvo, who was appointed in December 1998.

As an indication of the "must attend" status this dinner had attained, both Paul Cellucci, governor of Massachusetts, and Thomas Menino, mayor of Boston, were guests. Each extended welcoming remarks to the more than 800 fellow attendees. The cochairs of the gala were John M. "Jack" Connors Jr., CEO of the marketing communications firm Hill, Holliday, Connors, Cosmopulos, Inc., and Dennis J. Picard, CEO of the Raytheon Company. The dinner raised more

than $1.5 million, bringing to the total raised after 10 dinners to $13 million.

The Cardinals Encouragement Award was presented to Clementina and Joseph M. Chéry, representing the Louis D. Brown Peace Institute, in recognition of the courageous way they had transformed the tragic loss of their son into a quest for peace. Their son, Louis David Brown, was shot and killed on his way to a Christmas party given by a group called Teens Against Gang Violence, a violence prevention and peer leadership group. In honor of their son, they founded a center for peace education and support services for survivors of violence.

Background music for the evening featured the University Orchestra and the University Chorus, who capped off the night with a roundly applauded musical finale.

The 11th American Cardinals Dinner, Chicago
May 5, 2000

The 11th American Cardinals Dinner, the first for cohost Cardinal George, was held at the Chicago Hilton. Eight cardinals attended, including six resident cardinals: Cardinal Mahony, Cardinal Bevilacqua, Cardinal Keeler, Cardinal Maida, Cardinal Law, and Cardinal George. Cardinal Cahal Daly, archbishop of Armagh and Primate of All Ireland, and Cardinal Laghi, former nuncio to the United States, were also present. Also at the gala was current apostolic nuncio Archbishop Gabriel Montalvo. The archbishop of Washington, Cardinal James Hickey, was unable attend.

Prior to the dinner, the cardinals concelebrated a Mass at Holy Name Cathedral. Several days after the Chicago dinner, all of the American cardinals traveled to New York to attend the funeral of Cardinal John O'Connor, who had died on May 3.

The archdiocese of Chicago had five cochairs for the event: Sue Ling Gin, Jack Higgins, Harry M. Jansen Kraemer Jr., Monsignor Kenneth J. Velo, and Richard C. Notebaert, who represented the cochairs in welcoming the guests from the podium. The university leadership group included John P. Donohue, chairman of the Catholic University Board of Regents, and trustees Van P. Smith and Robert F. Comstock.

Cardinal George presented the American Cardinals Encouragement Award to Rev. Robert G. Casey, director of Casa Jesus. Elaine R. Walter, dean of the Benjamin T. Rome School of Music arranged for the entertainment provided by students of the Catholic University musical theatre program, featuring Mark Forrest.

Schools of The Catholic University of America

The Catholic University of America is unique as the national university of the Catholic Church and as the only higher education institution founded by the U.S. bishops. Established in 1887 as a papally chartered graduate and research center, the university began offering undergraduate education in 1904.

Catholic University consists of 12 schools. The University's anchors are the ecclesiastical schools of canon law, philosophy, and theology and religious studies. The School of Philosophy has the distinction of being one of the nation's oldest Ph.D. programs.

Established in January 2013, the School of Business and Economics brings the riches of the Catholic intellectual tradition and natural law to bear on business and economics.

Prominent among the nation's legal institutions is Catholic University's Columbus School of Law, a pioneer in clinical education and distinguished for offering one of the nation's broadest ranges of clinical experiences to students.

Undergraduate programs in the School of Arts and Sciences emphasize liberal arts education in a variety of subjects offered in the school's 18 departments.

Determining the Date of the Dinner

After years of trying to find a "set" date for the annual American Cardinals Dinner, early in Father O'Connell's tenure as president the following date-setting formula was agreed upon.

The Cardinals Dinner would fall on the fourth Friday of April of every year provided that it was two Fridays after Easter Sunday. If, in fact, the fourth Friday in April was only one Friday after Easter Sunday, the dinner would move to the first Friday in May.

Although it sounds complicated, that formula has worked, by and large, since 1998 except for the 16th, 24th, and 25th dinners for which the date was moved for specific reasons by the host archbishop/cardinal.

The 11th American Cardinals Dinner
Left to right, seated: Cardinals Daly, Keeler, George, and Law, and Archbishop Gabriel Montalvo.
Standing: Cardinal Laghi, Cardinal Bevilacqua, Father O'Connell, Cardinal Mahony, and Cardinal Maida..

Programs at all degree levels are offered in the School of Engineering. The school is known for teaching the latest concepts in biomedical, civil, electrical, and mechanical engineering.

The focus of the National Catholic School of Social Service is at the heart of the university's mission of service to the Church and the nation. NCSSS has a long-standing commitment to the poor, disenfranchised, refugees, and immigrants.

The School of Nursing is distinguished for consistently top-rated research-oriented programs.

Performance is emphasized at the Benjamin T. Rome School of Music, which presents more than 200 programs annually. It is Washington's only university music school.

The School of Architecture and Planning is the largest architecture school in the nation's capital. Students utilize the capital city as an "architecture laboratory" and take advantage of numerous foreign study programs as well.

The Metropolitan School of Professional Studies extends the educational resources of the university to nontraditional students in the Washington, D.C., region.

Cardinal John O'Connor
Archbishop of New York
B.A. 1951, Ph.D. 1952,
Ph.B. 1955

Cardinal John O'Connor Dies at Age 80

Archbishop of New York since January 1984, John J. O'Connor passed away on May 3, 2000, two days before The 11th American Cardinals Dinner. He had been a priest for 54 years, a bishop for 20 years, and a cardinal for 14 years. O'Connor attended The First American Cardinals Dinner in 1989 in Washington, D.C., and hosted the second in New York He also was at the cardinals dinners in Washington in 1994, Philadelphia in 1995, and Los Angeles in 1996.

Edward J. Pryzbyla, B.A. 1925, Catholic University Benefactor, Dies at Age 96

Eddie Pryzbyla was Catholic University's most generous benefactor. Seven months before his November 27, 2000, death he was at the groundbreaking for the building that would bear his name, the Edward J. Pryzbyla University Center. Three weeks before he died, he celebrated his 96th birthday on campus with Father O'Connell and others, in the president's dining room. On that occasion, he said, "I love Catholic University and have not missed a homecoming in 46 years." A saddened Father O'Connell considered it an honor to celebrate Eddie's funeral Mass in Chicopee, Mass., Pryzbyla's hometown.

The son of Polish immigrants, Pryzbyla graduated from Catholic University in 1925 with a B.A. in philosophy. He said his years at Catholic University were the best of his life. He entered the insurance industry after graduation, eventually forming his own business, centering on insurance, real estate, and finance. Quietly, he became financially successful. He married and was widowed twice,

Edward J. Pryzbyla and the cherry blossoms that abound on the campus that he spent a joyful lifetime beautifying.

The university had a special Eddie Pryzbyla Day in October 1986 to give the student body the opportunity to express their appreciation for his beautification efforts. Eddie said, "Students even learned to pronounce and spell my name."

Eddie Pryzbyla receiving an honorary degree from The Catholic University of America in 1995.

Eddie Pryzbyla at the groundbreaking for the new university center in April 2000. Although he knew the building would be named in his honor, he passed away before the center opened.

Father O'Connell and Eddie Pryzbyla strolling the campus. Pryzbyla had a yearly routine, usually in the spring, of visiting the campus and casting his expert eyes on existing shrubbery, trees, and flowers to determine his next beautification project.

with no children. His "children" were the students of Catholic University. Year after year he would return to the university he loved to enhance the beauty of the campus with an impressive array of plantings, flowerbeds, and trees in all parts of the property. His dedication to Catholic University was continuous, sincere, and extraordinary. The beautifully landscaped and tree-filled campus is one of the pleasing elements of the university, with the credit in large part going to Eddie Pryzbyla.

Years before his enormous support that made the student center possible, he was honored with the naming of Pryzbyla Plaza, the landscaped area between Shahan and McGivney halls, in front of Mullen Library. This was an area Pryzbyla particularly wanted to be at its picturesque best, with flowers and colorful plants to give the students a sense of pride in their university. But Eddie Pryzbyla will evermore be remembered for his final gift to his students and his university as the central benefactor in bringing into existence "The Pryz," the Edward J. Pryzbyla University Center.

Vincent P. Walter Jr.
B.A. 1969, M.A. 1973

Vincent P. Walter Jr. Dies at Age 62

Vincent P. Walter Jr., vice president, general secretary of the university, and secretary of the Board of Trustees, was killed by an automobile not far from the Catholic University campus on the afternoon of August 3, 2000. A longtime university staff member, he had been intimately involved with the planning for the cardinals dinner since its inception. Walter earned an undergraduate degree in 1960 and a master's in 1973, both from Catholic University. He was survived by his wife, Elaine, Ph.D. 1973, who was dean of the Benjamin T. Rome School of Music, their two children, Vincent III and Deanne, and three grandchildren.

Consistory of February 2001 (McCarrick, Egan, Dulles)

On February 21, 2001, Pope John Paul II named 44 new cardinals, including three Americans: Catholic University alumnus Theodore E. McCarrick, archbishop of Washington and Catholic University chancellor, Edward M. Egan, archbishop of New York, and Avery Dulles, S.J., the eminent theologian who taught at Catholic University for 14 years.

Cardinal Theodore McCarrick
Archbishop of Washington
M.A. 1960, Ph.D. 1963
CUA Staff, 1961–1965
CUA Chancellor, 2000–2006

Cardinal Avery Dulles, S.J.
American Theologian
CUA Faculty, 1974–1988

Cardinal Edward Egan
Archbishop of New York

The Columbus School of Law seen from the Pryzbyla Center.

The 12th American Cardinals Dinner
Left to right, seated: Cardinal McCarrick, Cardinal Maida, Archbishop Gabriel Montalvo, Cardinal George, and Cardinal Bevilacqua. Standing: Cardinal Keeler, Cardinal Mahony, and Father O'Connell, Cardinal Dulles, and Cardinal Law. Not pictured: Cardinal Egan and Cardinal Hickey.

The 12th American Cardinals Dinner, New York City
April 27, 2001

The 12th American Cardinals Dinner was the most successful to that point, raising more than $2 million for scholarship grants for deserving Catholic University students. Friends of Catholic University, from New York and elsewhere, flocked to the Waldorf Astoria Hotel to attend the first public event honoring three new United States cardinals, elevated by Pope John Paul II only two months earlier and all having close ties to New York and to The Catholic University of America. Cardinal Egan was archbishop of New York and a Catholic University trustee. The illustrious Jesuit theologian Cardinal Dulles was associated with Fordham University in New York City and had taught at Catholic University for 14 years. Cardinal McCarrick was a native New Yorker, archbishop of Washington, and Catholic University chancellor who had earned three degrees at the university. The cardinals concelebrated a Mass in St. Patrick's Cathedral before the dinner.

Left to right: Cardinals Bevilacqua, Maida, McCarrick, Mahony, and Keeler at St. Patrick's Cathedral, New York City, prior to the Mass preceding the dinner.

Cardinal Egan greeted the 1,100 guests at the dinner with great enthusiasm. A large corps of cochairs had worked for months to make the event a great success. Six came from the archdiocese: Florence D'Urso, James F. Gill, William F. Harrington, Thomas J. Moran, William F. Plunkett Jr., and Barry F. Sullivan. Three were from Catholic University: trustees Richard D. Banziger and Van Smith and the chairman of the Catholic University Board of Regents Peter D. Scudner. Tim Russert, moderator of *Meet the Press* was master of ceremonies and introduced Mayor Rudy Giuliani, who welcomed the assembly on behalf of the City of New York.

The Cardinals Encouragement Award was presented to the Sacred Heart Cultural Outreach Program, which provides an outstanding and all-encompassing after-school program for students, principally from Hispanic and African American families. Joanne Walsh, principal of Sacred Heart School, Bronx, accepted the award.

The presence at the dinner of 10 cardinals was another all-time high for an American cardinals dinner. In addition to the three recently elevated prelates, attending were the cardinal archbishops of Detroit, Chicago, Philadelphia, Boston, Baltimore, and Los Angeles, as well as the recently retired archbishop of Washington. Attendees could not recall when in the United States 10 cardinals were together at a charitable dinner for a single educational institution.

Terrorist Attack on the United States, 9-11-2001

As Catholic University students were hustling off to their morning classes on Tuesday, September 11, 2001, just before 9 a.m., four commercial airliners were hijacked by a well-organized group of terrorists. Three flew into buildings in suicide attacks on the cities of New York and Washington, D.C., resulting in almost 3,000 deaths.

Two of the hijacked planes rammed into the twin towers of the World Trade Center in New York. Within two hours, both towers collapsed, killing all inside, including hundreds of firefighters running up the stairs to provide help and hundreds of men and women running down trying to get out. The New York City fire department lost 340 firefighters, a chaplain, and two paramedics, the deadliest incident for firefighters in the history of the United States. The suicide terrorists flew one of the hijacked planes to Washington, D.C., crashing into the first floor level of the Pentagon building, causing severe damage. The fourth plane was heading for Washington, D.C., but the passengers on board attempted to overcome the terrorists and

the plane crashed into a field near Shanksville, Pa.

As word of the attacks spread, there was stunned amazement on the Catholic University campus. Everything stopped as television sets blared minute-by-minute happenings. The archbishop of Washington and Catholic University chancellor, Cardinal Theodore E. McCarrick, called Father O'Connell requesting that he and all students, faculty, and staff attend a Mass that afternoon at the Basilica. To a standing-room-only crowd, the cardinal delivered a stirring and mesmerizing homily ending with a call to prayer. At Catholic University and across the country, prayer, meditation, and contemplation prevailed as houses of worship were filled to overflowing with Americans attempting to grasp the scope of the tragedy. Virtually everyone was touched in one way or another by the events of 9/11. Thousands lost loved ones and everyone seemed to know someone who lost someone, or had a friend who knew someone who lost someone. The term "ground zero" entered the lexicon. The World Trade Center site became hallowed ground. Day after day Americans followed the anxious efforts of hundreds of people at ground zero moving debris, lifting and looking under girders, literally sifting dirt in the fruitless hope of finding survivors, finally just trying to at least find an identifiable body. It was a terrible time at The Catholic University of America and throughout America.

Frank G. Persico

Not long after the sudden death of Vincent Walter, Frank G. Persico became vice president for university relations and chief of staff in the Office

Frank G. Persico, B.A. 1974, M.A. 1976

of the President.

A double alumnus with undergraduate and graduate degrees, Persico had served in a variety of positions over the years, including executive director of alumni relations, dean of students, associate dean of the Columbus School of Law, and general secretary to the

After the 9/11 terrorist attack, Father O'Connell, the administration, faculty, and staff took every opportunity to counsel the student body, many of whom were personally affected by the tragedy. Pictured here are students jamming the atrium of the law school building a few days after 9/11 at one of the many seminars and gatherings conducted by faculty members intended to try to bring some sense to what happened.

Board of Trustees. In 2009 he received the Frank A. Kuntz '07 Award, which recognizes "unsung heroes" at the university. He was honored by the Holy See in 2008 with the Benemerenti Medal, which was instituted by Pope Gregory XVI in 1832 and is conferred on those who have exhibited long and exceptional service to the Catholic Church. Over his long and distinguished career, Persico has served six presidents and has helped design and direct most major university events — including Commencement, Convocation, and inaugurations; the visits of popes John Paul II, Benedict XVI, and Francis; the university centennial; and 125th anniversary celebration. He has played a principal role in many of the cardinals dinners since their inception.

Since 1980 only Brother Gregory Nugent, F.S.C., for whom Nugent Hall is named, until 1992, Vincent P. Walter Jr., from 1992 to 2000, and Frank Persico have held the key administrative posts of chief of staff to the president and secretary of the board of trustees.

Brother Gregory Nugent, F.S.C.

Vincent P. Walter Jr.
B.A. 1960, M.A. 1973

The 13th American Cardinals Dinner, Philadelphia

April 26, 2002

Held at The Wyndham Hotel in Philadelphia, The 13th American Cardinals Dinner was cohosted by Cardinal Bevilacqua and Father O'Connell. A native Philadelphian, the Catholic University president related how happy he was to be back in the city where he was born and raised.

The cardinals of the United States were under intense scrutiny at this time, having just returned from the Vatican where they were called on the carpet by Pope John Paul II to try to explain the revelations of the horrific clergy abuse of children, which burst full force into public knowledge in the Archdiocese of Boston in 2002. The public also learned that this abusive behavior by a small percentage of priests had been going on throughout the nation for years, with little or nothing being done by the hierarchy to stop it. It was further alleged that some bishops took action to cover it up. Cardinal Bevilacqua had the unpleasant task of facing intense questioning from reporters and camera people from 186 media outlets, after the Mass at the Cathedral Basilica of Saints Peter and Paul that preceded the dinner.

The Philadelphia dinner, with 800 guests, went on and was successful. Seven cardinals were present: Cardinal Keeler, Cardinal George, Cardinal McCarrick, Cardinal Law, and Cardinal Bevilacqua, as well as retired cardinals Hickey and Dulles, who was 84 years old. Also in attendance were Archbishop Gabriel Montalvo, apostolic nuncio, and Archbishop William Levada of San Francisco, a trustee of the university. Cardinals Maida, Mahony, and Egan were unable to attend. Cochairs of the event were Mr. and Mrs. H. Edward Hanway and Mr. and Mrs. Harold A. Sorgenti.

The Cardinals Encouragement Award went to one of the most innovative Catholic schools in the country, Saint Lucy Day School for Students with Visual Impairments. Sister Margaret M. Fleming, I.H.M., principal of the Upper Darby, Pa., school, accepted the award.

The proceeds of this dinner brought the amount of money raised for scholarships to $15 million.

The 13th American Cardinals Dinner
Left to right, seated: Archbishop Levada, Cardinal Dulles, Father O'Connell, Cardinal Hickey, and Archbishop Gabriel Montalvo. Standing, Cardinals Bevilacqua, McCarrick, Law, George, and Keeler.

With the archdiocese of Philadelphia becoming the fifth to have multiple dinners, the Catholic University trustees observed fatigue setting in among the clerical and lay leaders who had been asked to help organize these efforts. Seeking to continue the event in cities not having a red hat, several prelates who were members of the Catholic University Board of Trustees volunteered to host a dinner to relieve the pressure on those archdioceses that had borne the entire burden up to now.

Archbishop William J. Levada of San Francisco was present at the Philadelphia event in anticipation of his hosting the next dinner, the first to be planned in a city not led by a cardinal. Indeed, six of the ensuing nine American Cardinals Dinners were held in jurisdictions not led by a cardinal. They were San Francisco in 2003, Minneapolis in 2004, Miami in 2005, Las Vegas in 2007, Atlanta in 2010, and Phoenix in 2011.

An unintended, but pleasant consequence of this was the discovery that people in cities that rarely see a cardinal had extraordinary interest, enthusiasm, and, important for The Catholic University of America, excellent press coverage when the cardinals gathered for the yearly dinner.

The John K. Mullen of Denver Memorial Library

The 14th American Cardinals Dinner, San Francisco

May 2, 2003

Archbishop William J. Levada, a trustee of the university, was cohost with Father O'Connell of the 14th American Cardinals Dinner, held at the Fairmont San Francisco. This was the first dinner held in Northern California and the first in a diocese not led by a cardinal. (Less than three years after the dinner, Levada would be appointed a cardinal in the Roman Curia and named Prefect of the Congregation of the Doctrine of the Faith, the highest Vatican position ever held by an American.) The dinner was preceded by a Mass at the Cathedral of Saint Mary of the Assumption.

Present at the San Francisco gala were six of the seven resident cardinals: Cardinal McCarrick, Cardinal George, Cardinal Maida, Cardinal Mahony, Cardinal Bevilacqua, and Cardinal Keeler. The archbishop of New York, Cardinal Egan, was unable to attend. Also present was the former archbishop of Boston, Cardinal Law, who retired to Rome in December 2002. The apostolic nuncio, Archbishop Gabriel Montalvo, also was at the dinner, as were Bishop William E. Lori of Bridgeport, who was the chairman of the Catholic University Board of Trustees, and Archbishop Harry J. Flynn of St. Paul and Minneapolis, who concluded the proceedings with an invitation to the next year's dinner in Minneapolis.

The Cardinals Encouragement Award was presented

The 14th American Cardinals Dinner
Left to right, seated: Cardinals George, Keeler, Maida, and Bevilacqua, and Archbishop Gabriel Montalvo.
Standing: Cardinal Law, Cardinal McCarrick, Father O'Connell, Archbishop Levada, Bishop Lori, and Cardinal Mahony.

The John K. Mullen of Denver Memorial Library was rededicated on March 15, 2004, following a $6 million, three-year renovation program that completely updated the library. This building, a gift of John K. Mullen of Denver, president of the Colorado Milling and Mining Company, was constructed in 1925, with an addition in 1928.

to Saint Anthony Parish of North Fair Oaks, San Mateo County, which serves a predominantly Latin American community. Dinner cochairs were Robert Begley and Robert Craves and students from the Benjamin T. Rome School of Music again provided the entertainment, notable especially for a spectacular rendition of the "Star-Spangled Banner" sung by Catholic University seniors Kelly Faltus, Justin Heminger, and Julia Strukley. Members of the President's Society, a group of seniors who are selected to serve as members of the official staff of the Catholic University president's office, were on hand to escort honorees to the hall and to their tables as they were introduced.

Cardinal Justin Rigali
Archbishop of Philadelphia
S.T.B. 1961

Consistory of October 2003 (Rigali)

Pope John Paul II's ninth and final consistory was announced on September 28, 2003, and held on October 21. Thirty cardinals were named, including one American, Justin F. Rigali of Philadelphia, an alumnus of Catholic University.

The Edward J. Pryzbyla University Center Opens

No single event at Catholic University in the last century has had a greater effect on the university than the opening of the Edward J. Pryzbyla University Center, commonly known as "The Pryz." From the beginning, Father O'Connell referred to it as "the living room of Catholic University," and that is exactly what it has become. It is difficult to imagine Catholic University without it.

Dedicated on October 19, 2002, in connection with the alumni homecoming weekend, it was opened in early 2003 even though all the amenities were not in place. Father O'Connell sensed what the Pryzbyla Center would mean to future students and wanted the graduates of that year to personally experience the joyful effect of this building. For a good part of their time at Catholic University, these seniors had to endure many inconveniences, rearranging their walking habits to get around the center's construction site, for example, which was located in the precise center of the main campus.

The Edward J. Pryzbyla University Center cost $27 million and has 104,000 square feet of space. It houses the university dining facilities, with two dining halls, (when it opened dining services in three locations moved here), a convenience store, student offices, and ample conference and lounge space. This "student-friendly" building serves as the university's gathering space. It is three stories tall and as long as a football field. Conferences, major lectures, student fairs, and university parties are held in the Great Room. A noteworthy Great Room event occurred in 2008 when Pope Benedict XVI came to The Catholic University of America

A month before the Chicago dinner in May 2000 ground was broken for the new Edward J. Pryzbyla University Center, which changed life on campus.

At the time of the San Francisco dinner, the big news around the Catholic University campus was the enthusiastic reception given to the opening earlier in the year of "The Pryz"— the Edward J. Pryzbyla University Center.

Another view of The Pryzbyla Center.

to speak to Catholic educators. Events too large to be held inside, such as those celebrating the university's 125th Anniversary in 2012, take place on the patio and west lawn of The Pryz.

Eddie Pryzbyla, Catholic University class of 1925, was present for the April 2000 ground-breaking,

but passed away the following November, never seeing the completion of the major university facility that he made possible. For generations, Pryzbyla was an enthusiastic and consistent supporter of Catholic University, establishing a trust for the university and setting up an estate plan with the university as the beneficiary. This evolved into his enormous financial funding of the university center. Year after year Eddie made a steady stream of donations to enhance the beauty of the Catholic University campus, providing ideas, funds, materials, and in many cases manpower to plant hundreds of trees, bushes, and other decorative species in all parts of the campus. His desire to enhance the outdoor living space for students and visitors was extraordinary. After doing all he could to make the outdoor experience of the students better, he culminated his lifetime of generosity by making the construction of the university center a reality. It was more than fitting that the new facility be named the Edward J. Pryzbyla University Center.

The 15th American Cardinals Dinner, Minneapolis-St. Paul
April 23, 2004

The Twin Cities hosted The 15th American Cardinals Dinner, with the magnificent Cathedral of St. Paul the venue for the Mass prior to the dinner. Archbishop Harry J. Flynn of St. Paul and Minneapolis was principal celebrant, joined by the cardinal archbishops of Washington, Los Angeles, Baltimore, Detroit, Chicago, and Philadelphia. The dinner, held at the Hilton Minneapolis, raised almost $1 million, bringing the total raised for scholarships to Catholic University to more than $19 million since the dinner's inception.

Six cardinals were honored at the dinner, which was cohosted by Archbishop Flynn and Father O'Connell: Cardinal McCarrick, Cardinal Mahony, Cardinal Keeler, Cardinal Maida, Cardinal George, and Cardinal Rigali. The archbishop of New York, Cardinal Egan, was unable to attend. This was the first dinner for Cardinal Rigali of Philadelphia, who received a red hat in October 2003. Also in attendance was the chairman of the Catholic University Board of Trustees, Bishop William E. Lori of Bridgeport, and the apostolic nuncio Archbishop Gabriel Montalvo.

The Cardinals Encouragement Award went to the Dorothy Day Center, the largest and most comprehensive multiservice center for the homeless in St. Paul.

Clarence C. Walton,
Ph.D. 1950,
President, 1969–1978

Clarence C. Walton, 10th President, Dies at Age 88

Clarence C. Walton, president of The Catholic University of America from 1969 to 1978, died of pneumonia on April 13, 2004, at his home in Catonsville, Md. He was the first layman to lead the university and first to hold the title as president rather than rector.

A native of Scranton, he graduated from the University of Scranton and earned a master's degree from Syracuse University and a doctorate from The Catholic University of America. He completed postdoctoral work at the University of Geneva in Switzerland and at Harvard University. Walton served as a lieutenant in the U.S. Navy during World War II. Following military service he returned to the University of Scranton, serving as chairman of the Department of History and Politics from 1946 to 1953. He went on to become dean of Duquesne University's School of Business (1953–1958), associate dean at the Columbia University Business School (1958–1963), and dean of Columbia University's School of General Studies (1963–1969), before being named the 10th president of Catholic University in 1969.

Following his nine years at Catholic University, Walton taught and consulted in the field of ethics. A devout Catholic, he was survived by his wife of 57 years, Elizabeth Kennedy Walton, two children and five grandchildren. Mrs. Walton died on December 10, 2013, at the age of 93.

In 1989 one of the student residential units of Centennial Village was dedicated Walton House in honor of Catholic University's 10th president.

Cardinal James Hickey
Archbishop of Washington
S.T.L. 1946
CUA Chancellor, 1980–2000

Cardinal James Hickey Dies at Age 84

The 16th American Cardinals Dinner in Miami on January 28, 2005, took note of the passing of Cardinal James Hickey, retired archbishop of Washington, October 24, 2004. As chancellor of the university, Cardinal Hickey had enthusiastically supported the decision to mount these events and hosted the first in 1989 and fifth in 1994. He attended 10 consecutive dinners as archbishop of Washington and two after his retirement. When he passed away in 2004, he was 84 and had been a priest for 58 years, a bishop for 37 years, and a cardinal for 16 years.

The 15th American Cardinals Dinner
Left to right, seated: Cardinals Mahony, George, McCarrick, Keeler, and Maida. Standing: Bishop Lori, Archbishop Montalvo, Father O'Connell, Archbishop Flynn, and Cardinal Rigali.

An aerial view of campus, with the 49-acre West Campus on the left.

Catholic University Expands Holdings

Less than a week after the Minneapolis dinner, Father O'Connell and his associates celebrated the acquisition of a large parcel of land adjacent to the main campus. Located between Harewood Road and North Capitol Street, the purchase gives Catholic University the opportunity to create a grand entrance to the campus from one of Washington's main streets directly north of the United States Capitol.

In the mid-1990s, Catholic University's chancellor and archbishop of Washington, James A. Hickey, learned that the government was placing for sale a 49-acre parcel of land, part of the property of the Armed Forces Retirement Home, popularly called "the Old Soldiers Home." Catholic University and several developers immediately expressed interest. Since the site was adjacent to Catholic University property and therefore of enormous benefit to the university, several major political figures were informed, for it was the sale of government land, and they became actively involved on the side of the university. The issue dragged on for some time. In March 1999, less than a year after becoming Catholic University's president, Father

O'Connell, along with Robert F. Comstock, who was chairman of the finance committee of the Board of Trustees, a local attorney, and a Catholic University alumnus, travelled to Capitol Hill to testify before the Committee on National Security of the House of Representatives, which was holding hearings on the sale.

Father O'Connell's persistence, considerable negotiations, and the institution of land-use agreements led to an agreement five years later. The Armed Forces Retirement Home would sell the property to The Catholic University of America for a little over $22 million.

On April 29, 2004, Father O'Connell signed the papers and delivered the purchase price to acquire 49 acres of land, which Catholic University calls the West Campus. The property is immediately adjacent to the existing 144-acre campus, which was already the largest university campus in the District of Columbia.

This was the largest undeveloped parcel of land in the District of Columbia and dramatically increases the footprint of the university, broadly enhancing the possibilities for creative thinking regarding its use for years to come. At the time of the contract signing, Father O'Connell said,

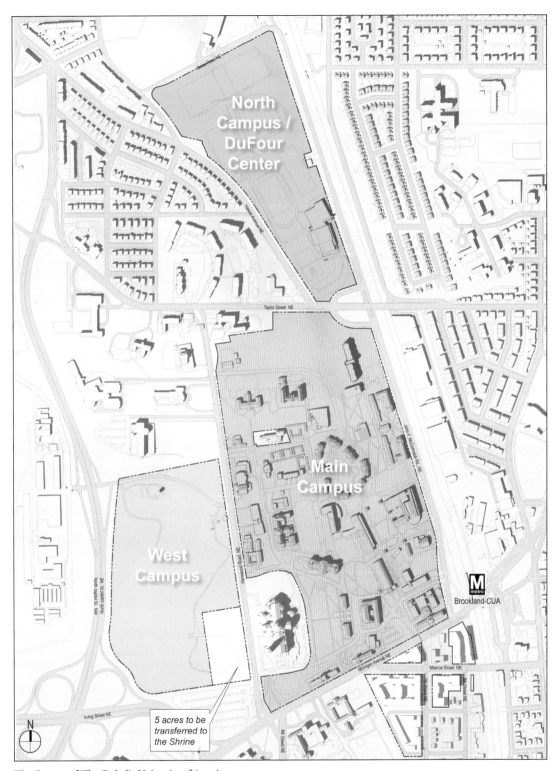

The Campus of The Catholic University of America

Map showing the 49-acre West Campus purchased in April 2004. The university sold 5 acres to the Basilica of the National Shrine of the Immaculate Conception in 2012. Catholic University has by far the largest campus of all educational institutions in Washington, D.C.

"This is an extraordinary milestone for Catholic University. It gives us ample room to expand for the next century. The acquisition will ensure that we continue to provide for our students, faculty, staff, and visitors a traditional campus and a beautiful 'green' oasis in the heart of the nation's capital."

The 16th American Cardinals Dinner, Miami
January 28, 2005

For the third consecutive year, the dinner was held in a city and cohosted by a trustee of the university — Archbishop John C. Favalora — who was not a cardinal. This pattern, established to relieve the pressure of organizing and hosting two or more dinners over a relatively short time, had proven successful. Having the dinners in areas of the country that rarely experience a visit from an individual cardinal makes the appearance of a half dozen or more a major event. A significant by-

product is the visibility and positive press coverage the university receives in areas that are unfamiliar with Catholic University.

Several years earlier, Father O'Connell had instituted a variety of initiatives to capitalize on the interest generated by the appearance of multiple cardinals. In advance of the Miami dinner, Catholic University admissions representatives contacted and in many cases personally visited the local Catholic high schools to talk about the university's virtues and encourage seniors to place Catholic University on their list of colleges to visit. In addition, an alumni reunion was held prior to the event and, on the afternoon of the dinner, the host archbishop and the Catholic University president held a press conference resulting in notable press coverage.

The Miami dinner was held at The InterContinental Hotel. Archbishop Favalora asked Father Pat O'Neill, an archdiocesan priest, to spearhead the effort, resulting in a highly successful enterprise. In addition, Father O'Connell added a new

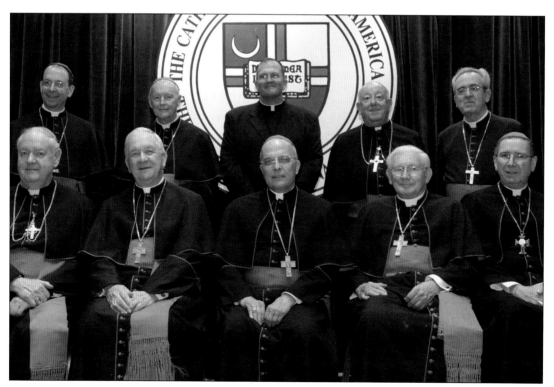

The 16th American Cardinals Dinner
Left to right, seated: Cardinals Egan, Maida, George, Keeler, and Mahony.
Standing: Bishop Lori, Cardinal McCarrick, Father O'Connell, Archbishop Favalora, and Cardinal Rigali.

On October 7, 1979, a year after his election at the age of 56, a vibrant Pope John Paul II visited Catholic University. At right is New Orleans Archbishop Philip H. Hannan, then chairman of Catholic University trustees.

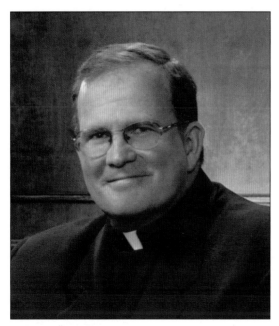

Father David M. O'Connell, C.M.

feature, having members of the President's Society, all senior undergraduates, act as emcees from the podium, providing commentary and introducing the speakers. This specially selected group of undergraduate seniors assists in the president's office and helps out with various university functions.

All seven resident cardinals attended, including Cardinal Mahony, Cardinal Keeler, Cardinal Maida, Cardinal George, Cardinal McCarrick, Cardinal Egan, and Cardinal Rigali. Also present

was the chairman of the Board of Trustees, Bishop William E. Lori of Bridgeport. The apostolic nuncio, Archbishop Gabriel Montalvo, who attended all dinners since becoming the papal ambassador to the United States in December 1998, was not well and could not attend. He was diagnosed with cancer, resigned as nuncio in December 2005, and died in August 2006.

The cardinals and other visiting clergy concelebrated a Mass earlier in the day at the Cathedral of Saint Mary. The Cardinals Encouragement Award was presented to The Marian Center, Miami.

Including the proceeds from this event, the annual dinners had cumulatively raised more than $20 million for scholarships at Catholic University.

On April 2, 2005, less than three months after the Miami dinner, the world was saddened by news of the death of Pope John Paul II. All the United States cardinals rushed to Rome for the funeral of the Holy Father, which was followed by the conclave that elected Joseph Cardinal Ratzinger, who took the name Pope Benedict XVI.

Pope John Paul II

remember the humble, wise, and fearless priest who became one of history's great moral leaders."

The Pope suffered from Parkinson's disease for more than a decade, but his youthful vigor was his hallmark for the early years of his papacy. He made scores of trips outside Rome, including five major visits to the continental United States in 1979, 1987, 1993 (for World Youth Day in Denver), 1995, and 1999, plus two stopovers in Alaska in 1981 (Anchorage) and 1984 (Fairbanks).

During the pontiff's first trip, he made a memorable October 7, 1979, visit to Catholic University, where he spoke to several hundred Catholic educators in what was then the gymnasium, now the Edward M. Crough Center for Architectural Studies.

At the time of his death, Pope John Paul II had appointed 115 of the 117 cardinals eligible to vote for his successor. The two appointed by Pope Paul VI were Cardinal William Baum of the United States and the future pope, Cardinal Joseph Ratzinger of Germany.

Pope John Paul II had named 231 cardinals worldwide, including the following 15 from the United States (in the order they were elevated)

Joseph Bernardin, Archbishop of Chicago

Bernard Law, Archbishop of Boston

John O'Connor, Archbishop of New York

James Hickey, Archbishop of Washington

Edmund Szoka, Archbishop of Detroit

Roger Mahony, Archbishop of Los Angeles

Anthony Bevilacqua, Archbishop of Philadelphia

William Keeler, Archbishop of Baltimore

Adam Maida, Archbishop of Detroit

J. Francis Stafford, Vatican Curia

Francis George, Archbishop of Chicago

Theodore McCarrick, Archbishop of Washington

Edward Egan, Archbishop of New York

Avery Dulles, S.J., the eminent American theologian

Justin Rigali, Archbishop of Philadelphia

Pope John Paul II Dies at Age 82

After a long period of failing health, Pope John Paul II died on April 2, 2005, ending a papacy of 26 years, six months. He was elected at the youthful age of 56 on October 16, 1978, beginning a history-making pontificate, third longest among popes, and leaving an indelible mark on the Church and the world. He was mourned worldwide by people of all levels of prominence. President George W. Bush said, "Pope John Paul II was an inspiration to millions, and to so many more throughout the world. We will always

Conclave Elects
Pope Benedict XVI
April 19, 2005

When John Paul II died on April 2, 2005, 117 cardinals were eligible to vote for a successor, two of whom were ill. Another 66 were over the age of 80 and not eligible to vote, for a total of 183 cardinals, the highest ever. The conclave opened on April 18, 2005. On the following day, after four ballots, they elected Cardinal Joseph Ratzinger of Germany, who was serving in the Roman Curia as head of the Congregation for the Doctrine of the Faith. He took the name Pope Benedict XVI.

A total of 115 cardinals entered the conclave — the most in history — including the following 11

Americans: William W. Baum, Bernard F. Law, Edmund C. Szoka, Roger M. Mahony, William H. Keeler, Adam J. Maida, J. Francis Stafford, Francis E. George, O.M.I., Theodore E. McCarrick, Edward M. Egan, and Justin F. Rigali. Two United States cardinals were over the age of 80 and not permitted to vote: Anthony J. Bevilacqua and Avery Dulles, S.J.

Consistory of March 2006
(Levada, O'Malley)

Pope Benedict XVI's first group of cardinals was named on February 22, 2006, with the consistory held on March 24. Fifteen cardinals were appointed. Two Americans received red hats: William J. Levada, in the Vatican curia, and Seán P. O'Malley, O.F.M. Cap., archbishop of Boston and an alumnus of Catholic University.

Cardinal William Levada
Vatican Curia

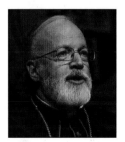

Cardinal Sean O'Malley,
O.F.M. Cap.
Archbishop of Boston
M.A. 1976, Ph.D. 1978
CUA Faculty, 1969–1973

Pope Benedict XVI Elected, April 2005

The 17th American Cardinals Dinner
Left to right, seated: Cardinals Baum, Maida, Keeler, Mahony, Egan, and Dulles.
Standing: Cardinal O'Malley, Cardinal Rigali, Bishop Lori, Father O'Connell, Cardinal McCarrick, and Archbishop Sambi.

The 17th American Cardinals Dinner, Washington, D.C.
April 28, 2006

In connection with the gathering in Washington for The 17th American Cardinals Dinner, Father O'Connell and the cardinals were invited to the White House that morning to meet with representatives of President George W. Bush to share with them the position of the Catholic Church on immigration reform and the needs of immigrants in general, and to receive a presentation from Karl Rove, the White House deputy chief of staff, on the Bush administration's position on that subject. At the morning meeting were cardinals McCarrick, Keeler, and Mahony, along with Father O'Connell.

Held for the third time in the nation's capital, the 2006 cardinals dinner took place at the Ronald Reagan Building and International Trade Center, cohosted by Cardinal McCarrick and Father

O'Connell. Seven of the eight resident cardinals were honored: Cardinal Mahony, Cardinal Keeler, Cardinal Maida, Cardinal Egan, Cardinal Rigali, Cardinal O'Malley (who had become a cardinal a month earlier), and Cardinal McCarrick. Two retired cardinals also were in attendance, Cardinal Baum and Cardinal Dulles. Also present was the chairman of the Catholic University Board of Trustees, Bishop William E. Lori of Bridgeport, and, at his first cardinals dinner, the recently appointed apostolic nuncio, Archbishop Pietro Sambi.

At the dinner, Father O'Connell brought the guests to their feet with the announcement that the Knights of Columbus had agreed to contribute $8 million to completely renovate Keane Hall, a three-story, 50-year-old building that sits in the middle of campus and had been vacant for many years. It would house the Pontifical John Paul II Institute for Studies on Marriage and Family, a graduate school of theology affiliated with Catholic University and the Pontifical Lateran University in Rome, and be

Father O'Connell awarding the Presidents Medal, the university's highest honor, to Smith Bagley at the 2006 American Cardinals Dinner.

renamed McGivney Hall. A life-size statue of the founder of the Knights of Columbus, Rev. Michael McGivney, was commissioned to stand outside the south entrance. Supreme Knight Carl Anderson is a Catholic University trustee.

At the dinner, Smith Bagley, the founder of the American Cardinals Dinner, was presented with the President's Medal, the university's highest honor. The model for these dinners, established by Bagley when he was head of the Catholic University Board of Regents and chairman of the first American Cardinals Dinner in 1989, has remained basically the same over the years.

At a Mass prior to the dinner in the Basilica of the National Shrine of the Immaculate Conception, Cardinal McCarrick was the principal celebrant, with Father O'Connell delivering the homily.

The Cardinals Encouragement Award went to the Little Sisters of the Poor, who operate the Jeanne Jugan Residence, a local facility for the elderly

poor named for the founder of the Little Sisters of the Poor.

Entertainment was provided by students in Catholic University's Musical Theatre Program.

Happenings On Campus

The aim of having all student residences on the main campus was proceeding well with the groundbreaking in March 2007, for the new 402-bed Opus Hall. Another initiative during the 2007–2008 school year was the launching of the Center for Global Education by Provost James Brennan. In the fall of 2008, Brennan and Father O'Connell traveled to Rome to dedicate offices and classrooms leased from St. John's University for the Rome portion of the program.

The 18th American Cardinals Dinner
Left to right, seated: Archbishop Sambi, Cardinal Maida, Bishop Pepe, Cardinal Rigali, and Bishop Lori.
Standing: Cardinal O'Malley, Cardinal Egan, Archbishop Wuerl, Father O'Connell, and Cardinal Mahony.

The 18th American Cardinals Dinner, Las Vegas
April 27, 2007

Five resident cardinals gathered for The 18th American Cardinals Dinner held in Las Vegas. The bishop of Las Vegas, Joseph A. Pepe, a Catholic University trustee, was cohost with Father O'Connell. Present were cardinals Mahony, Maida, Egan, Rigali, and O'Malley. Also in attendance was Donald W. Wuerl, the recently named archbishop of Washington and Catholic University chancellor; Bishop William E. Lori, chair of the Catholic University's Board of Trustees, and Archbishop Pietro Sambi, the apostolic nuncio. The dinner was held at the Four Seasons, Las Vegas. The Cardinals Encouragement Award went to Catholic Charities of Southern Nevada, which provides a wide range of social services to those in need.

Bishop Pepe and the visiting cardinals concelebrated a Mass earlier in the day in the Shrine of the Most Holy Redeemer, with Father O'Connell delivering the homily. Bishop Pepe said he enjoyed "this special occasion to celebrate a public Mass with the American cardinals, who gather here in the diocese of Las Vegas for the first time to raise money for Catholic University scholarships." He went on to say, "The Mass and dinner provide rare opportunities to see the cardinals gather in person, and we welcome this chance to join with them in support of students at the national university of the Catholic Church in America." The dinner raised $1.2 million, bringing the total raised to date for Catholic University scholarships to $22 million.

Opus Hall
Ground was broken in March 2007 for this student residence, which was occupied two years later. It is seven stories high, houses 402 students, and was the first in the District of Columbia to be a "LEED compliant" (Leadership in Energy and Environmental Design) residence hall. Neil J. Rauenhorst, B.Arch. 1976, and his wife, Becky, made a multimillion-dollar gift to Catholic University toward the construction of this facility. Given the opportunity to name the building, Rauenhorst, who at the time headed a company called The Opus Group, asked that it be named Opus Hall.

Consistory of November 2007 (Foley, DiNardo)

Pope Benedict's second consistory was held on November 24, 2007. Twenty-three cardinals were appointed, including two Americans, John P. Foley, a Philadelphia priest assigned for many years to the Vatican curia, who was appointed Grand Master of The Equestrian Order of the Holy Sepulchre of Jerusalem, and Daniel N. DiNardo, archbishop of Galveston-Houston, an alumnus of Catholic University.

Cardinal John Foley
Grand Master, Order of the
Holy Sepulchre

Cardinal Daniel DiNardo
Archbishop of
Galveston-Houston
B.A. 1971, M.A. 1973

Pope Benedict XVI visits The Catholic University of America

April 17, 2008

When word was received in the fall of 2007 that the Holy Father was to make his first (and what was to be his only) trip to the United States the following April, with The Catholic University of America among his stops, Father O'Connell, a member of the leadership group preparing for the visit, offered to have the Catholic University publications office design the official logo to appear on all documents and printed material. Catholic University's publications director, Donna Hobson, a talented graphic designer with more than 20 years experience, was assigned the task and worked assiduously on the project. She brought honor to Catholic University, for her creation was selected to be the official logo. When the submitted graphic was accepted by the Vatican, Hobson said she was "honored to have the opportunity to design something of such importance to the Church."

The papal airplane landed in Washington, D.C., on April 16. President George W. Bush delivered a singular honor to Pope Benedict XVI by greeting him personally at the airport upon his arrival. (The customary procedure is for the visiting dignitary to travel to the White House where the

Very Rev. David M. O'Connell, C.M., presented Donna Hobson with a framed copy of the official logo she designed for the 2008 papal visit of Pope Benedict XVI to the United States.

president would be waiting to greet him.) The next day the Holy Father was on the Catholic University campus enjoying the shouts of glee from enthusiastic students, faculty, staff, and invited guests. Father O'Connell, whom the Pope knew

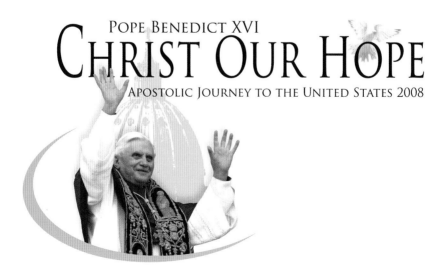

from prior meetings, escorted the Holy Father to the Great Room of the Edward J. Pryzbyla University Center. There, Pope Benedict XVI delivered an address on Catholic education to 400 Catholic educators, including the presidents of all Catholic universities in the United States.

The Pope greeting CUA students from the Popemobile.

Father O'Connell making a presentation to His Holiness.

On April 17, 2008, Pope Benedict XVI addressed Catholic educators in the Pryzbyla Center. Left to right: Pope Benedict XVI, and Very Rev. David M. O'Connell, C.M.

The 19th American Cardinals Dinner, Boston

April 25, 2008

As the cardinals gathered in Boston for The 19th American Cardinals Dinner, the feeling of euphoria was still in the air following the memorable visit of Pope Benedict XVI to Catholic University a week earlier. The campus had never looked better, and the atmosphere among all elements of the university family was positive. The several goals Father O'Connell established when he arrived as president were coming to fruition as he was approaching the 10-year mark of his presidency. When he began his tenure as president, Father O'Connell set out to create an aura of spirituality and Catholicity among the entire Catholic University community. His progress in this regard was notable in 2008, for observers said

that what started as "words and spoken intentions" had moved to the current observation that this was not "an aura," but an evident fact. He also intended to significantly enhance the on-campus experience of each student and to improve the physical fabric of the buildings and grounds.

All aspects of Father O'Connell's grand design were thriving. The beauty of the campus was earning the plaudits of students and visitors. Significant, too, were the improvements to existing structures and the new construction. The physical composition of the university campus improved in a startling fashion. With the construction of the 402-bed Opus Hall proceeding well, Catholic University would have during the 2008–2009 academic year, 19 residence halls, all on the main campus, including the venerable Gibbons Hall, which opened in 1912 and was undergoing renovations, remodeling, and updating. Over

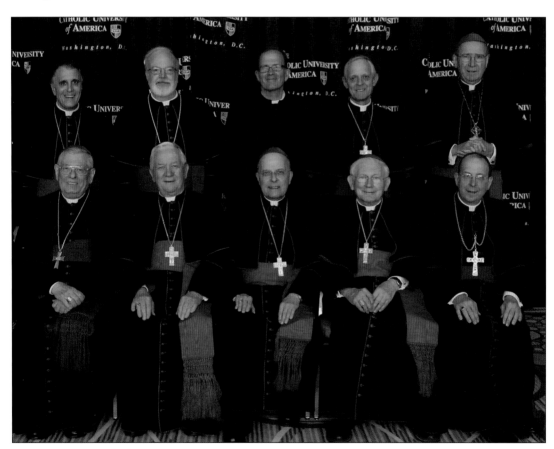

The 19th American Cardinals Dinner
Left to right, seated: Archbishop Sambi, Cardinal Maida, Cardinal George, Cardinal Keeler, and Bishop Lori.
Standing: Cardinal DiNardo, Cardinal O'Malley, Father O'Connell, Archbishop Wuerl, and Cardinal Mahony.

the past decade five new buildings had been erected and 20 other buildings undergone major renovations. Of course, the opening of "The Pryz," with its Food Court, a Starbucks, and a score of other amenities was the biggest hit. Also of major importance were the many improvements to the athletic facilities, including the installment of artificial turf on the football field. The opening of the beautifully restored McGivney Hall, in a central point of the campus, with its handsome and comfortable lobby and classrooms, added to the luster of the campus environment.

In the near future, the envisioned multimillion-dollar renovation of Cardinal Hall suggested more exciting things ahead. In addition, there were two long-term accomplishments of great significance: the acquisition of an additional 49 acres of mostly undeveloped land along Harewood Road and the development of the property previously called

South Campus, into Monroe Street Market.

The atmosphere was indeed positive as the memories of the papal visit started to fade and committees got into high gear and were reminded of how important it was to Catholic University that the 19th cardinals dinner, like those before, be a success. Cardinal O'Malley cohosted the dinner with Father O'Connell, which was held at the Renaissance Boston Waterfront Hotel. Cardinal O'Malley was principal concelebrant at the Mass, prior to the dinner, at the Cathedral of the Holy Cross, with Father O'Connell delivering the homily. The Cardinals Encouragement Award was presented to the Boston-run program Grandparents as Parents, which identifies and responds to the unique concerns of parenting grandparents and the children they are raising.

Attending his first cardinals dinner was the archbishop of Galveston-Houston, Cardinal Daniel DiNardo, who had become a cardinal the previous November. Also present were Cardinal Mahony, Cardinal Maida, Cardinal George, and the recently retired archbishop of Baltimore, Cardinal Keeler. Unable to attend were Cardinal Egan of New York and Cardinal Rigali of Philadelphia. Also in attendance was Archbishop Wuerl, Bishop Lori, and Archbishop Pietro Sambi. This was the third American Cardinals Dinner held in Boston.

Cardinal O'Malley at the podium

The Knights of Columbus and The Catholic University of America

Virgil C. Dechant
Former Supreme Knight

In keeping with their generous support to Catholic University since its inception, in 1989 under Supreme Knight Virgil C. Dechant, a Catholic University trustee, the Knights of Columbus was a principal contributor to The First American Cardinals Dinner. The order has continued its support of the dinner ever since.

It is difficult to overstate the amount of financial aid and encouragement the Knights of Columbus (K of C) has provided to The Catholic University of America since the early years of both.

The Knights of Columbus was founded in 1881 and The Catholic University of America six years later. In 1899, the university proposed the establishment of a K of C chair in American History at Catholic University. This hit a resonant chord with the Knights, for they were very desirous to have all Catholics, and indeed everyone, know the true story of the development of the Catholic

Church during early days of this nation. The public school history books at that time contained outrageous anti-Catholic commentary and the K of C was a leading force in having the Church treated fairly. In 1904, more than 10,000 knights and their families attended a massive ceremony at Catholic University where a check for $55,633.79 was presented to establish this chair.

Generations later, in 1965, the Knights established an ongoing K of C Scholarship Fund providing a portion of tuition for sons and daughters of Knights.

In 1914, Graduate Hall, now called Father O'Connell Hall, was opened on Michigan Avenue, designed as a companion to Gibbons Hall. (Originally called Graduate Hall, then University Center, then Cardinal Hall, and finally, in June 2010 renamed Father O'Connell Hall in honor of Very Rev. David O'Connell, C.M., 14th Catholic University president, 1998–2010.) It initially housed graduate students and was built with funds contributed by the Knights of Columbus. The K of C membership raised $500,000 between 1909 and 1913, to create a permanent endowment for Catholic University fellowships for graduate history students, with a preference for Knights and their families. Keane Hall had housed the university's first Knights of Columbus Fellows. Eminent Catholic historian, John Tracy Ellis, M.A. 1928, and Provost Emeritus C. Joseph Nuesse, Ph.D. 1930, (who also wrote a history of the university's first 100 years), were K of C Fellowship Students at Catholic University.

In 1989, as Catholic University celebrated the 200th anniversary of the creation of the American Church in conjunction with the 100th anniversary of the university, the Knights of Columbus established the $2 million Bicentennial of the United States Hierarchy Fund at Catholic University. Earnings from this fund have been paying for university projects each year since.

In 2008, long-vacant, five-story Keane Hall, located in the heart of campus, underwent an $8 million refurbishment paid by the K of C and was renamed McGivney Hall in honor of its founder, who it is speculated will one day likely be proclaimed a saint.

Left to right: At the dedication of McGivney Hall, Bridgeport Bishop William E. Lori, Knights of Columbus Supreme Chaplain; Carl A. Anderson, Supreme Knight; Washington Archbishop Donald W. Wuerl; and Very Rev. David M. O'Connell, C.M., CUA president.

The Catholic University law school and the K of C also have an intimate relationship. The Columbus School of Law, founded by the Order, merged with Catholic University in 1954. The Columbus School of Law was an outgrowth of the nationwide program begun in 1919 by the Knights of Columbus to provide free education to veterans returning after World War I. By 1939, this law school had the third largest enrollment in the United States with 1,059 students. In 1954, an act of Congress signed by President Dwight D. Eisenhower approved the merger of the Columbus School of Law with The Catholic University School of Law to form the present Columbus School of Law of The Catholic University of America, which is currently located in a $32 million state-of-the-art facility completed in June 1994.

The Knights of Columbus has made many additional contributions to the area surrounding Catholic University, but one deserves note. In 2011, the K of C established the Shrine of Blessed John Paul II in the former home of the Pope John Paul II Cultural Center, located adjacent to the recently purchased 49-acre West Campus, across Harewood Road from Main Campus. Previously located here was the Augustinian House of Studies. When the Augustinian community moved, Catholic University acquired the property, later making

it available to the prime movers of the project dedicated to the Holy Father. The building on this 12-acre site was torn down and up went the beautiful $65 million Pope John Paul II Cultural Center, which opened in March 2001. The center suffered years of financial difficulties; the K of C came to the rescue and acquired the facility, renaming it, and establishing a new focus. When the Holy Father was declared a saint in 2014, the facility became the Shrine of Saint John Paul II.

The Catholic University of America Council 9542 has been an active Knights of Columbus Council on campus since the 1980s. The group was named Outstanding College Council during the 2014 Knights of Columbus College Councils Conference in New Haven, Conn.

McGivney Hall

Rev. Michael J. McGivney
Founder

Named for the Rev. Michael J. McGivney, founder of the Knights of Columbus, McGivney Hall was dedicated on September 8, 2008. The Knights of Columbus financed the $8 million renovation of the building

Carl A. Anderson
Supreme Knight

formerly called Keane Hall. The building now houses the Pontifical John Paul II Institute for Studies on Marriage and Family, a graduate school of theology affiliated with both Catholic University and the Pontifical Lateran University in Rome. The North American branch of the institute was opened at Catholic University in 1988 with funding from the Knights of Columbus. Current Supreme Knight Carl A. Anderson, a Catholic University trustee, was the institute's first vice president and dean. McGivney Hall is a five-story building in the center of the campus. The first floor has a handsome and comfortable lobby and classrooms. The second and third floors have faculty and staff offices. It also houses the 120-seat Keane Auditorium, retaining the name of Catholic University's first rector, Archbishop John Joseph Keane. Outside the building is a life-sized statue of Father McGivney.

The Basilica of the National Shrine of the Immaculate Conception

As with the university itself, the Knights of Columbus has played a major role in the development and success of the Basilica. In 1959 the edifice was dedicated, with the K of C contributing $1 million for the construction of the 329-foot campanile, called the Knights' Tower. Four years later, Catholic University's chancellor, Archbishop Patrick O'Boyle of Washington, blessed the 56-bell carillon installed in the Knights' Tower and financed by the Order. In 2007, the K of C paid for the installation of a magnificent 3,780-square-foot mosaic in the ceiling of the tower, called the Incarnation Dome. It depicts the mysteries of the life of Christ. It is difficult to calculate the amount of additional support the Basilica of the National Shrine of the Immaculate Conception has received from the Knights of Columbus.

The Basilica of the National Shrine of the Immaculate Conception sits on land contributed by Catholic University years ago. Originally it was envisioned to be a university church. Cardinal James Gibbons, Catholic University chancellor, laid the cornerstone in 1920. As plans developed it was decided that it become a national church erected in honor of the Immaculate Conception, the patroness of Catholic University and the nation. Although not officially part of the university, the Basilica dome is visible from all parts of the campus. Also, with Masses, Commencement, and special university events routinely held here, students, parents, and friends consider it part of the Catholic University environment.

Cardinal Avery Dulles, S.J.
American Theologian
Faculty, 1974–1988

Cardinal Avery Dulles, S.J., Dies at Age 90

Rev. Avery Dulles taught at The Catholic University of America for 14 years, from 1974 to 1988. Dulles said, "My years at Catholic University have been as happy and productive as any comparable period of my life." Students taught by Dulles have commented on his kindness and consideration of everyone as much as on his brilliance and intellectual prowess. When Father Dulles was named a cardinal by Pope John Paul II in 2001, he was almost 83 and asked not to be ordained a bishop. He died on December 12, 2008, at 90 and was a priest for 52 years and a cardinal for seven. Dulles attended the American Cardinals Dinners in 2001, 2002, and 2006.

Welcoming The Knights of Columbus

In its 100th year, the Catholic University welcomed the Knights of Columbus. Enlisting over 100 members in its 1st year, the Knights quickly became one of the most active groups on campus.

The Knights of Columbus were not totally new to Catholic University, however. The Columbus School of Law was one result of the Knight's concern for education. The bell tower of the Shrine of the Immaculate Conception stood as a symbol of the Knight's devotion to the Catholic Church and many of our students owed their opportunity for education in a Catholic environment to scholarships provided by the K of C.

In this sense, Catholic University was only formally welcoming the Knights of Columbus, whose presence was felt ever more strongly as they forever strived to increase their role of service to the campus community.

Chivalry is not dead yet. These young men are happy at the prospect of being the first members of the CUA Chapter of the Knights of Columbus. Photo by Mickey Sullivan.

This graphic from the 1989 Catholic University Yearbook contains a photo of several charter members of Catholic University Knights of Columbus Council # 9542.

Left to right, front row: Frank Nolan, Father John Orr, (unknown). Rear row: (unknown), Father Frank, Robert Iannone, Lance Barry, (unknown), Michael Lally, Roy Zimmerman, Thomas Gallagher, (unknown), Father Reilly, (unknown), Joe McGinty, (unknown), Father Stephen Hayes, O.P. Thomas Gallagher was the first Grand Knight and Michael Lally the second. Father Frank Donio, S.A.C., was the president of the Catholic University Alumni Association Board of Governors from 2013 to 2014.

The 20th American Cardinals Dinner, Houston

April 24, 2009

Houston's beautiful new Sacred Heart cocathedral was the site of the Mass preceding The 20th American Cardinals Dinner, concelebrated by visiting cardinals, bishops, and priests.

"On Friday afternoon," as Cardinal O'Malley put it, "I made a lightning trip to Houston for the annual cardinals dinner to raise scholarship money for Catholic University. The evening started with a Mass at the new cathedral in Houston. This was the first time I was in the new cathedral and I was impressed. Archbishop Joseph Fiorenza built it toward the end of his tenure as bishop of Galveston-Houston. And, of course they not only have a new cathedral but they also have a new cardinal. Cardinal Daniel DiNardo presided at the Mass and Father O'Connell preached a very inspiring homily."

The next morning, Cardinal O'Malley caught the first flight back to Boston for an important meeting. The Boston archbishop's effort to ensure he attended the dinner is indicative of the continuous support the United States cardinals have given to Catholic University since its founding, punctuated by their support and interest since the initiation of these cardinals dinners in 1989.

All five resident United States cardinals attended the Houston dinner, traveling from Los Angeles, Chicago, Philadelphia, and Boston, joining the dinner cohost Cardinal DiNardo, archbishop of Galveston-Houston. Three retired cardinals traveled to Houston from Detroit, Baltimore, and New York. Also, the chairman of the Catholic University Board of Trustees came from Washington, D.C., as did the apostolic nuncio and the Catholic University president.

At the dinner, Father O'Connell spoke fondly of Cardinal Dulles. During a visit to the campus after becoming a cardinal, Dulles had said, "The years at Catholic University were among the happiest of my life."

Almost $1.5 million was raised for scholarships at this dinner and press coverage was expansive.

The 20th American Cardinals Dinner
Left to right, seated: Archbishop Fiorenza, Cardinal Keeler, Cardinal Maida, Cardinal Egan, and Archbishop Wuerl. Standing: Cardinal O'Malley, Cardinal Mahony, Cardinal DiNardo, Father O'Connell, Cardinal Rigali, and Cardinal George.

The Vatican ambassador to the United States, officially called the apostolic nuncio, Archbishop Pietro Sambi, conveys the regards of Pope Benedict XVI to the guests at the Houston dinner.

Father O'Connell, president of CUA since 1998, delivering the homily at the Mass preceding the dinner.

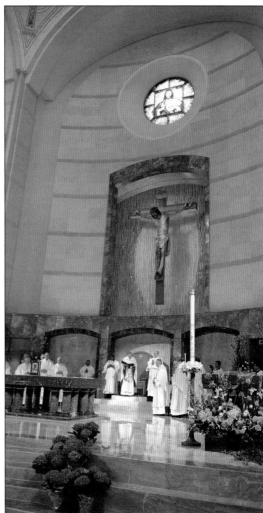

The Mass prior to the dinner was held in the beautiful, newly dedicated Sacred Heart cocathedral.

The people of Houston, a principal Southwest city, Catholic and not, enjoyed reading about and seeing eight Princes of the Church, joining collaboratively in supporting and applauding the national Catholic university.

In Houston, 700 guests attended the dinner, which was held at the Hyatt Regency Houston. Among that number were students from Catholic University who spoke about their experience at the university. The American Cardinals Encouragement Award was presented to Sister Maureen O'Connell, the executive director of Angela House, a transitional housing facility in Houston for women recently released from prison,

to assist them in their return to every-day living.

Galveston-Houston became a "two city" diocese because of the importance during the 1800s of the port city of Galveston, and the desire to retain its name after the move of the central administration of the diocese to the more populated city of Houston. There are cocathedrals in both cities. The Diocese of Galveston, the first in Texas, was created in 1847, and changed to Galveston-Houston in 1959.

A month after this dinner, Monsignor William A. Kerr, a key person intimately involved with the start of these dinners, passed away. He had been vice president for university relations during the presidency of Father William J. Byron, S.J., and had been challenged with the task in 1989 of organizing the first American Cardinals Dinner. It was an enormous success. He then established the machinery to carry the event forward on an annual basis.

C. Joseph Nuesse, Ph.D. 1944, Dies at Age 95

C. Joseph Nuesse
Ph.D. 1944

On May 5, 2009, C. Joseph Nuesse (pronounced "niece") died. He earned a doctorate in sociology at Catholic University as a Knights of Columbus fellow, remaining on campus for half a century as a faculty member, dean, provost, executive vice president, and consultant. A prolific writer, at the time of the celebration of the 100th Anniversary, he wrote *The Catholic University of America: A Centennial History.*

Monsignor William A. Kerr
S.T.L.1966

Monsignor William A. Kerr, S.T.D. 1966, Dies at Age 68

Monsignor William A. Kerr was vice president for university relations when preparations began for Catholic University's centennial. He had the task of recruiting key individuals from across the country to be formed into the first Board of Regents, from which came the idea to have an annual American Cardinals Dinner. He created the dinner organizational plan, which basically has remained unchanged over the years. He left Catholic University to become president of Pittsburgh's LaRoche College, where he served for a dozen years. Monsignor Kerr suffered a massive stroke as he was celebrating Mass on May 15, 2009, and died shortly thereafter. A close friend was quoted as saying, "For a man who gave his life to the Church, that's a pretty sweet way to go."

Cardinal DiNardo and cocelebrants at the Mass preceding The 20th American Cardinals Dinner in Houston.

Smith Bagley, Founder of The American Cardinals Dinner

Smith Bagley Dies at Age 74

Smith W. Bagley, second chairman of the Board of Regents of Catholic University and "founder" of the American Cardinals Dinners, died January 2, 2010, in Bethesda, Md. The cause was a stroke he suffered Christmas Eve, said his wife, Elizabeth Frawley Bagley, who was ambassador to Portugal during the Clinton administration. An heir to the R. J. Reynolds tobacco fortune, Bagley spent much of his time in philanthropic and public affairs work. In addition to being chairman of the Board of Regents of The Catholic University of America, he served on the board of the John F. Kennedy Center for the Performing Arts.

Smith Walker Bagley was born on April 1, 1935, in Manhattan and grew up in Greenwich, Conn., the son of Henry and Nancy Reynolds Bagley. His grandfather, Richard Joshua Reynolds, founded the R. J. Reynolds Tobacco Company in 1875. Besides his wife of 26 years, Bagley was survived by six children and five grandchildren. He received the Catholic University President's Medal at the 2006 American Cardinals Dinner in Washington, D.C.

The 21st American Cardinals Dinner, Atlanta
April 23, 2010

Very Rev. David M. O'Connell, C.M., announced several months before the Atlanta dinner that he would be stepping down following the current semester. This was the 12th cardinals dinner cohosted by Father O'Connell. Archbishop Wilton D. Gregory of Atlanta, a university trustee, was cohost for this event held at the Hyatt Regency Atlanta. The cochairs were Tammy and Jim Eckstein, Sally and Frank Hanna III, and Shirley and Mike Trapp. Mayor Kasim Read joined Archbishop Gregory in welcoming the assembled guests to the city of Atlanta. The Mass prior to

the dinner was held at the Cathedral of Christ the King.

Nine prelates attended The 21st American Cardinals Dinner, including four cardinals and five archbishops: Cardinals George, DiNardo, Maida, and Egan; archbishops Wilton D. Gregory, Donald W. Wuerl (who was to become a cardinal several months after this dinner), Allen H. Vigneron, Pietro Sambi, and retired archbishop of Atlanta, John F. Donoghue.

In his remarks at the Atlanta dinner, Archbishop Gregory spoke about the importance of Catholic University to the Church, "This exceptionally fine institution has provided scholarships and research opportunities for so many different areas of Church life. Its goal is to strengthen ecclesial life in our country by educating men and women for positions of leadership and public service, always in conformity with our Catholic faith."

The 21st American Cardinals Dinner
Left to right, seated: Retired Archbishop Donoghue, Archbishop Sambi, Cardinal Maida, Cardinal Egan,
and Archbishop Vigneron. Standing: Archbishop Wuerl, Cardinal DiNardo, Archbishop Gregory, Father O'Connell, and
Cardinal George.

Archbishop Gregory concelebrating Mass in the Cathedral of Christ the King with visiting cardinals,
bishops, and priests prior to the Atlanta dinner.

Continuing the policy of moving the dinners to cities not accustomed to seeing multiple cardinals, for the fifth time the dinner was held in a city not led by a cardinal. Archbishop Gregory was fearful of adhering to the custom of charging $1,000 per plate for the dinner, for this would be the first time anyone could recall an event in Atlanta going that high. However, the event was again a success, with more than 400 guests attending and more than $1 million raised. Since these annual functions began, more than $25 million had been raised to bolster student scholarships at The Catholic University of America.

A sad note was Father O'Connell's moving comments on the passing of the founder of these yearly dinners, Smith Bagley, who had died the previous January. It was Bagley, chairman of the Catholic University Board of Regents, who recommended to then Catholic University president, Rev. William J. Byron, S.J., and to the university Board of Trustees that an annual American Cardinals Dinner be held. Bagley was chairman of the first dinner held on December 12, 1989, in Washington, D.C.

Very Rev. David M. O'Connell, C.M., Steps Down

Father O'Connell, president of Catholic University since 1998, announced in October 2009 that he was stepping down as president the following August.

On June 4, 2010, the apostolic nuncio, Archbishop Pietro Sambi, announced that Pope Benedict XVI had appointed Father O'Connell as coadjutor bishop of the Diocese of Trenton. He succeeded as the 10th bishop of Trenton on December 1, 2010. Father O'Connell's 12 years is second longest in the history of The Catholic University of America, a half-dozen years short of the 18-year tenure of Bishop Thomas J. Shahan, who served as fourth rector from 1909 to 1927.

The look of the campus in 2010 was much different from the time of Father O'Connell's arrival. It was beginning to change toward the end of Father Byron's 10 years of leadership in 1992

Bishop David M. O'Connell, C.M.
Catholic University President, 1998–2010
Bishop of Trenton since 2010

and continued to evolve during the six-year regime of Brother Patrick Ellis. However, it was during Father David O'Connell's 12-year administration that the final dramatic transformation took place, with the construction of the Edward J. Pryzbyla University Student Center, the renovation of McGivney Hall (formerly the long vacant Keane Hall), the improvements to the DuFour athletic complex, and the construction of three new student residences.

In addition there were the many projects not obvious to the visitor walking around the campus, including the renovation and upgrading of the Mullen Library, the renovation of the North Dining Hall into the Eugene I. Kane Health and Fitness Center, the creation of a "gateway building" with the gutting and remodeling of Cardinal Hall, renamed Father O'Connell Hall, and the upgrading of every other building on campus. Two additional campus alterations were the acquisition of the 49-acre property to create the West Campus and the transformation of what was the South Campus into Monroe Street Market.

In looking back on the legacy of a departing

Father O'Connell Hall

president, physical improvements, the bricks and mortar, are tangible measurements of success. Establishing a Catholic identity, which is most evident by the lack of it, is not, and therefore difficult to judge. When Father O'Connell arrived at Catholic University he perceived the lack of a Catholic identity and set his sights on its correction. As he was ending his presidency, Father O'Connell said: "Everything good for the university had to be rooted in a strong sense of Catholic identity, since we were and remain the national university of the Catholic Church in our country." That he clearly achieved his goal became evident to all and was best expressed by the comment of Catholic University chancellor, Archbishop Donald W. Wuerl, "Reinvigorating the university's Catholic identity is one of the signal achievements of Father O'Connell's tenure."

Father O'Connell Hall

At a Board of Trustees meeting shortly after Father O'Connell announced he would be leaving, the trustees voted to change the name of Cardinal Hall

to Father O'Connell Hall to commemorate his 12 splendid years at the helm of Catholic University. The change was formalized at a farewell dinner in Father O'Connell's honor in June 2010.

One of the most imposing buildings on campus, it was originally called Graduate Hall when it opened in 1914. It was designed as a companion to Gibbons Hall. The facility underwent a variety of name changes over the years as its function changed. In the summer of 2005, Father O'Connell announced his intention to completely renovate and restore the building, which had been vacant since the Edward J. Pryzbyla University Center opened in 2003. Father O'Connell Hall houses offices relating to student needs, including admissions and financial aid. The Office of Alumni Relations is also located there in the Craves Family Alumni Center, which was dedicated April 13, 2012. It is located on the ground floor of Father O'Connell Hall, once home to the well-known gathering place for students called The Rathskeller, affectionately known as "The Rat."

CHAPTER FOUR

Chapter Four

John Garvey
Catholic University President
2010–Present

John Garvey, Catholic University President 2010

ather O'Connell announced in October 2009 that he would be stepping down as president in the summer of 2010. On June 15, 2010, it was announced that John Garvey, 62, dean of Boston College Law School since 1999, was to be appointed the new president of The Catholic University of America, effective July 1, 2010. He was formally inaugurated as 15th president on January 25, 2011.

President Garvey was born September 28, 1948, in Sharon, Pa., the second of nine children. He met his wife, Jeanne, at Harvard. They married in 1975. They have five children.

A 1970 graduate of Notre Dame, he received his J.D. from Harvard Law School in 1974. He is a nationally renowned constitutional law expert. He was a professor at the University of Kentucky College of Law from 1976 to 1994, visiting professor at the University of Michigan Law School from 1985 to 1986, and professor at Notre Dame Law School from 1994 to 1999. He was the dean of Boston College Law School from 1999 to 2010, when he became president of The Catholic University of America.

From the start of the Garvey administration, Archbishop Donald Wuerl, Catholic University chancellor, provided enthusiastic support and encouragement to the new president. with both looking forward to the formal ecclesiastical inauguration in the Basilica of the National Shrine of the Immaculate Conception in January 2011. In October, the news arrived of the election of the chancellor to the College of Cardinals, which added a new dimension to the inauguration ceremony.

Left to right: In Rome at the reception at North American College following the November 2010 consistory are Frank Persico, vice president for university relations and chief of staff; President John Garvey; newly created Cardinal Donald W. Wuerl, archbishop of Washington and Catholic University chancellor; and Monsignor Kevin Irwin, dean of the School of Theology and Religious Studies at Catholic University at the time.

Consistory of November 2010 (Burke, Wuerl)

The third consistory in the reign of Pope Benedict XVI was held on November 20, 2010. Twenty-four cardinals were appointed, including two United States prelates, Raymond Leo Burke in the Vatican curia, and the archbishop of Washington, Donald W. Wuerl. Both have philosophy degrees from The Catholic University of America.

Cardinal Raymond Burke
Vatican Curia
B.A. 1970, M.A. 1971
Basselin Scholar

Cardinal Donald Wuerl
Archbishop of Washington
B.A. 1962, M.A. 1963
Basselin Scholar
CUA Chancellor, 2006–present

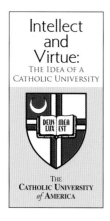

Inauguration of the New President

January 25, 2011

The theme of Garvey's inauguration was "Intellect and Virtue: The Idea of a Catholic University." The theme was extended throughout the spring semester with programming devoted to intellect and to virtue, including the following:

- A series of lectures on the interplay between virtue and their scholarly work by prominent intellectuals in disciplines, such as history, music, literature, and science.

- A four-month, university-wide campaign to encourage Catholic University students, faculty, and staff to reflect on the four cardinal virtues of prudence, justice, fortitude, and temperance.

- A conference on campus featuring scholars and presidents of universities from around the world on April 11–12, 2011, that explored the inaugural theme, particularly the ways in which virtue shapes how we learn and what we learn.

Garvey has vigorously promoted the Catholic intellectual tradition and has taken every opportunity to make students more aware of their faith. The dual concepts of intellect and virtue have been the resounding theme of his administration.

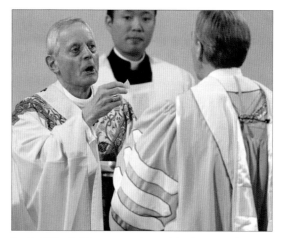

Cardinal Wuerl giving communion to John Garvey at the inauguration Mass.

The close friendship between the new president and the new cardinal was evident as John Garvey and Cardinal Wuerl greet one another following the formal inauguration ceremony.

The 22nd American Cardinals Dinner, Scottsdale, Ariz.

May 6, 2011

Many of the top leaders of the Catholic Church in the United States were in the Diocese of Phoenix for The 22nd American Cardinals Dinner to raise scholarship funds for The Catholic University of America. Bishop Thomas J. Olmsted of Phoenix, a member of Catholic University's Board of Trustees, cohosted the dinner, held at the Hyatt Regency at Gainey Ranch, Scottsdale, with President Garvey, the first layman in more than a quarter of a century to lead the university and only the third overall.

Preceding the dinner, Bishop Olmsted was principal celebrant of a Mass at St. Bernard of Clairvaux Church, also in Scottsdale, attended by the cardinals being honored at the dinner. In attendance were Cardinal George, Cardinal Rigali, Cardinal O'Malley, and Cardinal DiNardo and retired cardinals Egan and Mahony. The fifth resident cardinal, recently elevated Cardinal Wuerl,

had a prior engagement in Rome and could not attend. Also present were Archbishop Sambi and Archbishop Vigneron. Archbishop Sambi, who attended all six American Cardinals Dinners since becoming nuncio in December 2005, passed away 10 weeks after the Scottsdale dinner, on July 27, 2011.

Catholic University alumni in Arizona numbered more than 400 in 2011, with more than two dozen students from Arizona attending the university. Several of those students were featured in a video about the school presented at the dinner. The vicar general of the Diocese of Phoenix, Rev. Fred Adamson, said, "The University is hoping to build a greater awareness in the Southwest of the excellent Catholic academics and formation they offer to young people. The proceeds from the Cardinals Dinner will provide new opportunities for students from the southwestern United States to attend the university."

The Scottsdale dinner raised more than $900,000 for Catholic University scholarships. Since its inauguration, the annual event had raised more

The 22nd American Cardinals Dinner
Left to right, seated: Archbishop Vigneron, Cardinal Mahony, Cardinal Egan, and Archbishop Pietro Sambi.
Standing: Cardinal O'Malley, Cardinal Rigali, Bishop Olmsted, President Garvey, Cardinal George, and Cardinal DiNardo.

than $26 million to support scholarships for Catholic University students. The success of the Scottsdale dinner can be attributed to the splendid committee assembled by Bishop Olmsted comprising Shellie and Rick Andreen, Nancy and William Bidwell, Deb and James Campbell, Roger Debonis, Mary and Arthur DeCabooter, Melissa and John Fees, JoAnn Holland, Dawn and John Kelly, Sandie and Fred Mapp, Kathleen and Victor Smith, and Donna Marino.

A poignant photo of Archbishop Pietro Sambi, apostolic nuncio to the United States, addressing the Scottsdale gathering. He passed away less than three months after this picture was taken.

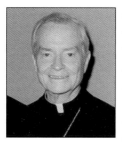

Philip M. Hannan
Archbishop of New Orleans
J.C.D. 1950

Archbishop Philip M. Hannan Dies at Age 98

Archbishop Hannan, a native of Washington, D.C., became a United States Army chaplain during World War II and was an auxiliary bishop of Washington from 1956 to 1965 when he became archbishop of New Orleans. He died on September 11, 2011, at the age of 98.

Hannan Hall was named after this Catholic University alumnus, former chairman of the Board of Trustees and close friend of the university.

Cardinal Anthony Bevilacqua
Archbishop of Philadelphia

Cardinal Anthony Bevilacqua Dies at Age 88

Anthony J. Bevilacqua hosted two cardinals dinners, in 1995 and 2002, in Philadelphia. He was very supportive of the university and these annual dinners, having missed attending only one of 12 functions from the time he became a cardinal in June 1991 until he retired in June 2003. When he passed away on January 31, 2012, Cardinal Bevilacqua was 88. He had been a priest for 62 years, a bishop for 31 years, and a cardinal for 20 years.

Guests enjoying the evening at the Scottsdale event.

Bishop Thomas J. Olmsted of Phoenix, (center) concelebrated Mass with the visiting cardinals, bishops, and priests at St. Bernard of Clairvaux Church, Scottsdale, prior to The 22nd American Cardinals Dinner.

Consistory of February 2012
(O'Brien, Dolan)

The fourth consistory of Pope Benedict XVI, who was two months shy of his 85th birthday, witnessed Edwin F. O'Brien, Grand Master of the Order of the Holy Sepulchre, and Catholic University alumnus Timothy M. Dolan, archbishop of New York, among the 22 prelates becoming cardinals.

Cardinal Edwin O'Brien
Grand Master, Order of the
Holy Sepulchre

Cardinal Timothy Dolan
Archbishop of New York
M.A. 1981, Ph.D. 1985

A smiling President John Garvey applauding the CUA students who took part in the festivities.

Left front: John and Jeanne Garvey at the Mass preceding the dinner.

Celebration of Catholic University's 125th Anniversary
April 2012

In May 2011, immediately following The 22nd American Cardinals Dinner, President Garvey set his sights on the university's commemoration of its 125th Anniversary on Founders Day, April 10, 2012.

To their joy, students were principal players in the endeavor, resulting in a collective feeling of "student spirit," and an increased love for their school, for one another, and for the administration.

A major component of the celebration, indeed its hallmark, was the Cardinal Service Commitment. President Garvey and the anniversary committee challenged the university community, including students, faculty, staff, and alumni, to perform 125,000 hours of service between the kick-off day, May 15, 2011, and Founders Day, April 10, 2012. The students erected a large thermometer at Pryzbyla Center and recorded the progress of the effort. By mid-September, the thermometer stood at 63,000 hours of service. By the end of January 2012, the goal of 125,000 service hours was surpassed, with the only question remaining, "How high will we go?"

During the celebratory year, each school of the university conducted an anniversary event featuring lectures, conferences, campus history walking tours, and other events. On continuous display in the May Gallery of Mullen Library was an exhibition that featured items tracing the development of the academic programs over the years and historic photographs and commentary on the music school, the residence halls, and the university's athletic accomplishments. In February, the Benjamin T. Rome School of Music presented a musical revue.

One of the concluding events of Founders Week was an anniversary Mass of Thanksgiving in the Crypt Church of the Basilica on April 10, celebrated by Cardinal Wuerl, followed by a gala outdoor student party on the West Lawn of the Pryzbyla Center. President Garvey commended

the assembled Catholic University community, "In your efforts you far exceeded the ambitious 125,000-hour goal we set for the university. In fact, the students, staff, faculty, and alumni of Catholic University performed 352,627 hours of service since we began collecting hours last May, I am both astonished by and proud of this show of gratitude and generosity."

Students concluded Founders Week on the evening of April 13 with the 125th Anniversary Founders Ball, held in a gigantic tent set up outside Mullen Library.

Catholic University alumni celebrated the university's founding on campus beginning with the dedication of the Craves Family Alumni Center on the afternoon of Friday, April 13. The new home of the Office of Alumni Relations is located in Father O'Connell Hall where The Rathskeller was located and provides much easier access for alumni, who for years had to ascend to the 4th floor of McMahon Hall with no elevator access.

On Saturday the alumni celebrated a Mass in Caldwell Hall Chapel, followed by a reception in the Pryzbyla Center Atrium. The 125th Anniversary Alumni Awards Dinner took place in the Pryzbyla Center Great Room. There the James Cardinal Gibbons Medal, the highest honor bestowed by the Alumni Association was presented to Kevin Ryan, B.A. 1989, president of Covenant House, a nationwide network based in New York dedicated to saving homeless kids.

On May 14, 2012, the university held its 125th Annual Commencement. Degrees were granted to more than 1,500 students. Delivering the Commencement address was the Honorable John Boehner, Speaker of the House of Representatives.

The final event related to the 125th anniversary, a four-day symposium marking the 50th anniversary of the Second Vatican Council, took place in late September. Hosted by Catholic University's School of Theology and Religious Studies, the symposium, Reform and Renewal: Vatican II after Fifty Years, attracted 400 participants from around the United States. Keynote speaker was Cardinal William Levada, prefect emeritus of the Congregation for the Doctrine of the Faith and a former Catholic University trustee.

The Students Had A Ball

Chart being revealed on Founders Day, April 10, 2012, displaying the final total of service hours, 352,627, almost triple the goal of 125,000 hours established a year earlier. Left to right: Cochairs Dean Randall Ott, School of Architecture and Planning; Bart Pollock, Office of Public Affairs; President Garvey, and Vice President and Chief of Staff Frank Persico.

President Garvey cuts a cake on Founders Day to celebrate the university's 125th anniversary as Randy Ott and Bart Pollock, cochairs of the anniversary committee, look on.

Frank Persico, vice president for university relations, delivers greetings at the gala outdoor student party on the West Lawn of the Edward J. Pryzbyla University Center.

The Craves family Alumni Center, located on the ground floor of Father O'Connell Hall, was dedicated as part of the celebration of the 125th Anniversary of CUA. This new construction resulted from the generosity of trustee emeritus Robert E., Graves, B.A. 1965; his wife, Gerri; and their daughter, Stacie Moore. Left to right: Cutting the ribon are Thomas Zoeller, B.A. 1985, then president of the alumni association, Gerri and Robert Craves, President John Garvey, and Cardinal Donald Wuderl, chancellor.

President Garvey speaks to students, faculty, staff, and alumni who gathered to celebrate Catholic University's 125th anniversary.

Robert E. Craves, B.A. 1965, addresses those assembled at the dedication of the Craves Family Alumni Center.

The 23rd American Cardinals Dinner
Left to right, seated: Archbishop Vigano, Cardinal Dolan, Cardinal DiNardo, and Cardinal Mahony.
Standing: Cardinal Wuerl, President Garvey, Cardinal George, and Cardinal O'Malley.

The 23rd American Cardinals Dinner, Chicago
April 27, 2012

President Garvey traveled to Chicago to cohost his second American Cardinals Dinner, and the 23rd overall, with Cardinal George at the Hilton Chicago Hotel.

Commenting on the event, Garvey said, "This dinner, an annual fund-raiser for Catholic University, has raised more than $27 million since 1989 to assist academically qualified students who are in need of financial support. We are tremendously grateful for these gifts, and for the opportunities they create for our students."

This was the third American Cardinals Dinner in Chicago. The first was cohosted by Cardinal Joseph Bernardin in 1992 and the other two by Cardinal George, in 2000 and 2012.

President John Garvey addressing the guests at The 23rd American Cardinals Dinner in Chicago.

Cardinals begin to line up for the receiving line at the Chicago dinner.

Cardinal Francis George, O.M.I., in the Cathedral of the Holy Name, delivering the homily at the Mass prior to the Chicago dinner.

Cardinal George at The 23rd American Cardinal Dinner, presenting the inaugural Cardinals Appreciation Award to Christine and Richard Guzior for their ongoing support of the Archdiocese of Chicago and many other Church activities.

Cardinal George was the main celebrant and homilist at the earlier Mass at Holy Name Cathedral. Six cardinals were at the dinner, including all five resident prelates from the archdioceses of Chicago, Boston, Galveston-Houston, Washington, and New York City, as well as the retired archbishop of Los Angeles. Cardinal George presented the Cardinals Appreciation Award to Richard and Christine Guzior for their ongoing support, in both time and resources, to the Archdiocese of Chicago and to a variety of other Church endeavors. This was the first award of this type to be presented, replacing the Cardinals Encouragement Award, which was last given in 2009.

Consistory of November 2012 (Harvey)

Pope Benedict XVI surprised everyone when he named a second group of cardinals in the same year, elevating six new red hat recipients on November 24, after appointing 22 in February 2012. One American was among the six, James M. Harvey, ordained for the archdiocese of Milwaukee in 1975, who has spent virtually his entire priesthood in service to the Vatican, most recently as Prefect of the Papal Household. Also elevated was Catholic University alumnus Luis Tagle, archbishop of Manila, Philippines. From 1987 until 1991, he studied theology at Catholic University, where he obtained a doctorate in theology, summa cum laude.

After five consistories in seven years, Pope Benedict XVI had named 90 cardinals, 74 of them electors and 16 over the age of 80. Nine were from the United States: William J. Levada, Seán P. O'Malley, O.F.M. Cap., John P. Foley, Daniel N. DiNardo, Raymond Leo Burke, Donald W. Wuerl, Edwin F. O'Brien, Timothy M. Dolan, and James M. Harvey.

Cardinal James Harvey
Vatican Curia

Cardinal Timothy Dolan, archbishop of New York and president of the United States Conference of Catholic Bishops, was the Commencement speaker in May 2012 and received a roar of understanding from the graduates when he said, "I am a proud alumnus having left here 30 years ago and just finished paying for my tuition." Cardinal Dolan is shown here displaying to the graduates the vestments of a new cardinal.

President John Garvey at 2012 Baccalaureate Mass.

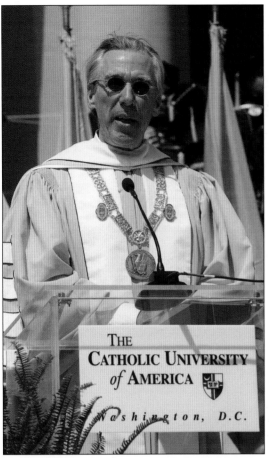

President John Garvey at the May 2012 Commencement.

Brother Patrick Ellis, F.S.C.
President, 1992–1998

Brother Patrick Ellis, F.S.C., 13th President, Dies at Age 84

Brother Patrick Ellis, F.S.C., president of The Catholic University of America from 1992 to 1998 died of acute leukemia at a nursing home for the Brothers of the Christian Schools in Lincroft, N.J., on February 21, 2013. A graduate of Catholic University, summa cum laude, he was the first religious brother to hold the position of Catholic University president. Before his leadership period at Catholic University, Brother Ellis had a 15-year tenure as president of LaSalle University, the longest in that university's history. As president of Catholic University, he dedicated the new $33 million building for the Columbus School of Law and was responsible for the installation of a multimillion-dollar project to enhance the campus computing infrastructure and complete the fiber-optic wiring for a high-speed computer network. A national leader in higher education, Brother Ellis was the cohost, with the resident cardinal, of six American cardinals dinners.

Pope Benedict XVI Resigns

Pope Benedict XV stunned the world in early February 2013, stating his intention to resign the papacy at the end of that month. The 85-year-old pope announced his decision during a meeting of Vatican cardinals, saying, "After having repeatedly examined my conscience before God, I have come to the certainty that my strengths due to an advanced age are no longer suited to an adequate exercise of the Petrine ministry."

He went on to say, "In today's world, subject to so many rapid changes and shaken by questions of deep relevance for the life of faith, in order to govern the barque of St. Peter and proclaim the Gospel, both strength of mind and body are necessary, strength which in the last few months, has deteriorated in me to the extent that I have had to recognize my incapacity to adequately fulfill the ministry entrusted to me."

Knowing that the option to resign was specific in the Code of Canon Law, Pope Benedict said, "Well aware of the seriousness of this act, with full freedom I declare that I renounce the ministry of bishop of Rome, successor of St. Peter, entrusted to me by the cardinals on 19 April 2005, in such a way, that as from 28 February 2013, at 20:00 hours, the See of Rome, the See of St. Peter, will be vacant and a conclave to elect the new supreme pontiff will have to be convoked by those whose competence it is."

The Pope specified that when his resignation became effective he would not take part in the conclave for the election of his successor and would temporarily move to the papal residence in Castel Gandolfo. His intention was to live permanently in a monastery inside the Vatican, which formerly housed cloistered nuns, when renovation work on the facility was complete. The Holy Father eventually moved there, as he put it, "for a period of prayer and reflection."

Pope Benedict was the first pope to resign in almost 600 years.

Newly elected Pope Francis being congratulated by Pope Emeritus Benedict XVI.

Pope Benedict at Catholic University in April 2008. The pontiff resigned the papacy February 28, 2013.

Pope Francis Elected
March 13, 2013

Following the resignation of Pope Benedict XVI, Cardinal Angelo Sodano, dean of the College of Cardinals, made preparations for the conclave. Entering the Sistine Chapel on March 12, 2013, to vote for the successor to Pope Benedict XVI were 115 cardinal electors who, a day later, on the fifth ballot, elected Jorge Mario Bergoglio, S.J., archbishop of Buenos Aires, who took the name Francis. The cardinal from Argentina was the first pope from Latin America and the first Jesuit.

The 2013 Conclave

Countries of origin of cardinals participating in the papal conclave of 2013 were Italy (28), the rest of Europe (32), North America (20, including 11 from the United States under the age of 80 and eligible to vote), South America (13), Africa (11), Asia/Oceania (11). Eligible but not attending the conclave were cardinals from Indonesia and Scotland.

United States cardinals at the conclave were Daniel DiNardo, archbishop of Galveston-Houston; Timothy Dolan, archbishop of New York; Francis George, O.M.I., archbishop of Chicago; Donald Wuerl, archbishop of Washington; Seán O'Malley O.F.M. Cap., archbishop of Boston; Roger Mahony, retired archbishop of Los Angeles; Justin Rigali, retired archbishop of Philadelphia; Edwin O'Brien, grand master of the Equestrian Order of the Holy Sepulchre; Raymond Burke, head of the Apostolic Signatura; James Harvey, archpriest of the Basilica of St. Paul Outside the Walls; and William Levada, retired prefect of the Congregation for the Doctrine of the Faith.

Eight of the 11 voting cardinals are alumni of The Catholic University of America: DiNardo, B.A. 1971, M.A. 1973; Dolan, M.A. 1981, Ph.D. 1985; George, M.A. 1965; Wuerl, B.A. 1962, M.A. 1963; O'Malley, M.A. 1972, Ph.D. 1978; Mahony, M.S.W. 1964; Rigali, S.T.B. 1961; and Burke, B.A. 1970; M.A. 1971.

Pope Francis.

The 24th American Cardinals Dinner, Washington, D.C.

May 10, 2013

The 2013 dinner, attended by 650 guests, was held at the Washington Hilton hotel. It was the fourth time the American Cardinals Dinner had been held in the nation's capital (previous dinners were in 1989, 1994, and 2006). Honored at the gala were three heads of archdioceses — cohost Cardinal Wuerl, Cardinal O'Malley, and Cardinal Dolan — as well as two retired archbishops — Cardinal McCarrick and Cardinal Rigali. Also attending were Archbishop Carlo Maria Vigano, apostolic nuncio, and Allan H. Vigneron, archbishop of Detroit and chairman of the Catholic University Board of Trustees. Dinner cochairs were Sandra Andreas McMurtrie and Robert F. Comstock.

Preceding the dinner was a Mass at the Cathedral of St. Matthew the Apostle, concelebrated by a large group of visiting cardinals, bishops, and clergy.

Cardinal Wuerl, Catholic University chancellor, presented the Cardinal's Appreciation Award to Thomas and Glory Sullivan for their dedicated commitment to the Archdiocese of Washington. In addition, Robert F. Comstock received the Distinguished Service Award for his long service to Catholic University. A graduate of the university and a member of its Athletic Hall of Fame, Comstock has served several terms as a member of the Board of Trustees, assisted each of the last four Catholic University presidents behind the scenes (including providing legal guidance in the acquisition of the 49-acre West Campus), was intimately involved with The First American Cardinals Dinner in 1989, and has contributed to each dinner since. President Garvey remarked, "No one is more deserving of this award than Bob Comstock." Present at the 24th dinner, as he was for the first in 1989 and all but one or two since, was Frederick R. Favo. An alumnus, emeritus trustee, generous benefactor, and enthusiastic supporter of the university, Favo has been a firm believer that these dinners have been of enormous

The 24th American Cardinals Dinner
Left to right, seated: Archbishop Vigano, Cardinal McCarrick, Cardinal Rigali, and Archbishop Vigneron.
Standing: Cardinal Dolan, Cardinal Wuerl, President Garvey, and Cardinal O'Malley.

The cardinals concelebrating Mass at the Cathedral of St. Matthew the Apostle prior to the dinner.

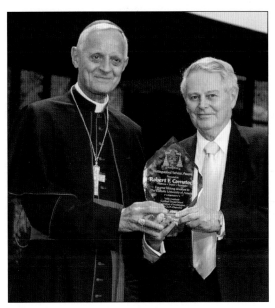

Cardinal Donald Wuerl presenting the Distinguished Service Awasrd to Robert F. Comstock for his many and varied contributions to the Archdiocese of Washington and The Catholic University of America.

At the conclusion of the 24th dinner Cardinal Dolan invited everyone to the Silver Anniversary American Cardinals Dinner the next year in New York City.

Standing with Tom and Glory Sullivan, recipients of the Cardinals Appreciation Award, are trustee emeritus Andrea Roane and Cardinal Wuerl.

benefit to the university, not only for raising $30 million for scholarship aid to deserving students, but also for bringing the message of The Catholic University of America, the nation's university for Catholics, to all parts of the country, year after year. He has been one of the consistent participants, and a true hero of the annual cardinals dinners.

At the conclusion of the dinner Cardinal Dolan announced that he looked forward to greeting everyone present, along with many New Yorkers, the next year at the 25th American Cardinals Dinner at the Waldorf Astoria Hotel.

With the $1.7 million raised at this dinner, the second largest in the history of these events, the dinners had raised more than $30 million for scholarships at Catholic University for deserving students from all parts of the country. The success of the American Cardinals Dinner not only permitted hundreds of worthy students to attend the university, it also enhanced the image of the university nationwide.

Edmund D. Pellegrino, M.D.
President, 1978–1982

Edmund D. Pellegrino, M.D., 11th president, Dies at Age 92

Dr. Edmund Daniel Pellegrino, president of The Catholic University of America from 1978 to 1982, died on June 13, 2013, nine days before his 93rd birthday. He was the second layman to hold the position of Catholic University president.

After graduating from New York's St. John's University, summa cum laude, he earned a medical degree from the New York University College of Medicine. Following military service with the Air Force, Pellegrino had a distinguished career in medical education and research. He was, in succession, professor and chairman of the department of medicine at the University of Kentucky and at the State University of New York at Stony Brook, then chancellor of the Center for

Health Sciences at the University of Tennessee. Prior to becoming president of Catholic University, he was president and chairman of the board of directors of Yale-New Haven Medical Center.

During Pellegrino's time as president, Pope John Paul II made his historic visit to Catholic University and addressed a large contingent of Catholic educators. An outstanding administrator, he was known for the camaraderie he established on campus among students, faculty, and staff.

Pellegrino followed his service as Catholic University president with another illustrious career specializing in the field of medical ethics, serving as chairman of the President's Council on Bioethics under the 43rd United States President, George W. Bush. The author of more than 600 published articles and chapters on medical science, philosophy, and ethics, he founded and directed Georgetown University's Center for Clinical Bioethics, which early in 2013 was renamed the Edmund D. Pellegrino Center for Clinical Bioethics.

Pellegrino and his wife, Clementine, had seven children and numerous grandchildren.

Robert E. Craves, B.A. 1965

Robert E. Craves, University Trustee 1998–2009, Dies at Age 72

Robert E. Craves, an alumnus, university trustee for a dozen years, and generous supporter of the university, died November 5, 2014. A founder of Costco Wholesale Corp, Craves was a great advocate for equal access to higher education. He cofounded the College Success Foundation to provide college scholarships to low-income, high-potential students. The Craves Family Alumni Center was named to acknowledge the extraordinary generosity to The Catholic University of America of Craves, his wife, Gerri, and their daughter, Stacie Moore. He was a committed supporter of The American Cardinals Dinner and was cochair of the 14th dinner in San Francisco in 2003.

The 25th American Cardinals Dinner, New York City

May 30, 2014

The Silver Anniversary American Cardinals Dinner was celebrated at the Waldorf Astoria Hotel, Friday, May 30, 2014, cohosted by Cardinal Dolan and President Garvey. This was the third time the dinner was held in New York City. The second cardinals dinner, in 1991, was cohosted by Cardinal John O'Connor and the 12th by Cardinal Edward Egan in 2001.

Eight American cardinals attended the dinner, including the five active archbishops of New York, Boston, Chicago, Washington, and Galveston-Houston. Also attending the black-tie event were Archbishop Carlo Maria Vigano, apostolic nuncio to the United States, and Archbishop Allen Vigneron of Detroit, chairman of the Catholic University Board of Trustees.

In his greeting President Garvey said, "It is an honor to cohost the dinner with Cardinal Dolan. We are proud to have him as an alumnus of The Catholic University of America. He has been a big supporter of the university and its mission. Just two years ago Cardinal Dolan gave an inspiring speech to our graduates at commencement. We deeply appreciate his generosity in cohosting this fundraising dinner to help our students obtain their goal of a Catholic University education." Garvey also acknowledged the presence of his predecessor as Catholic University president, Bishop David M. O'Connell, C.M., of Trenton.

Cardinal Dolan, who earned a doctorate in American Church history at the university, noted the unique role that Catholic University has for the Church in this country. "Daily I meet proud and grateful alumni of Catholic University," he said in his welcoming remarks. "Catholic University has a special history as the university founded by

The 25th American Cardinals Dinner
Left to right, seated: Archbishop Vigano, Cardinal McCarrick, Cardinal George, Cardinal Egan, Cardinal Rigali, and Archbishop Vigneron. Standing, left to right: Cardinal Wuerl, President Garvey, Cardinal Dolan, and Cardinal DiNardo. Missing from the picture, but present at the dinner is Cardinal O'Malley.

Cardinals processing to begin the Mass in St. Patrick's Cathedral the afternoon of The 25th American Cardinals Dinner. The Cathedral was undergoing renovation at the time of the dinner.

the bishops of the United States, I am proud to be an alumnus, and it is a joy to be able to serve as cohost of this 25th annual scholarship dinner. The university's mission to God, Church, and country is carried through its graduates — among them priests, men and women religious, corporate executives, public servants, teachers, scholars, and Broadway performers."

The cochairs of the dinner's leadership committee were Richard Banziger, Bill and Maryanne McInerney, and Jim and Jeanne Moye. Journalist Charlie Rose, who served as master of ceremonies, called upon Rosanna Scotto, the popular news anchor of WNYW's *Good Day New York*, and a graduate of Catholic University, to introduce the recipient of the Cardinal's Appreciation Award, Thomas J. Moran, president, chairman and CEO of Mutual of America.

Moran, a product of local archdiocesan schools, and a major benefactor of many church organizations and institutions, including Catholic University, said, "Catholic education allows every child to achieve his or her potential."

Rosanna Scotto told the story of how Moran was unable to speak when he entered the first grade of parochial school. She joked, "The nuns worked with him and by the time he was in second grade, he was talking, and talking, and he hasn't stopped talking since!" Moran thanked the assembled guests and said, "We all know that our faith is strongest when it is an educated faith. We can thank the Catholic system for that education, and The Catholic University of America is the symbol for all of us for Catholic education and great education."

As with all 25 American Cardinals Dinners, entertainment was provided by students and recent graduates of the Benjamin T. Rome School of Music. They delivered a spectacular show, including a medley of songs and sketches relating to New York.

Earlier in the day, Cardinal Dolan was principal celebrant and homilist at a 4:30 p.m. Mass at St. Patrick's Cathedral. Visiting cardinals, bishops, and clergy concelebrated the liturgy. The Mass was held during a period when the cathedral

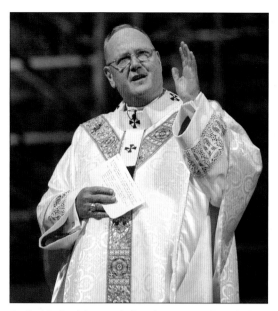

Cardinal Dolan delivering the homily in St. Patrick's Cathedral.

Television personality Charlie Rose was master of the ceremonies.

Cardinal O'Malley addressing the group.

Dinner chair Richard Banziger, CUA alumnus and former trustee, welcoming guests.

A view of the Waldorf Astoria dinner guests, with CUA music school students and recent alumni performing a medley of songs about New York at the Silver Anniversary gala.

John Garvey and Cardinal Dolan with Tom Moran, CEO of Mutual of America, who received the Cardinals Appreciation Award, and Rosanna Scotto, a local news anchor and CUA alumnus, who introduced Moran at the dinner.

was undergoing a multiyear renovation process with scaffolding covering the main body of the edifice including the entire sanctuary. In his homily Cardinal Dolan expressed his admiration for Catholic University, happily recounting his Catholic University pedigree. Cardinal Dolan was cheerful, upbeat, and smilingly welcoming to the Catholic University alumni and friends in attendance. Few of Cardinal Dolan's early career experiences bring him as much joy as his memories of happy and fruitful days as a student there. In a spiritually uplifting talk, the cardinal centered on the enormous contribution of the university to the Church and nation for more than a century and a quarter. In addition to his active involvement at the Friday Mass and dinner, on Thursday evening, Cardinal Dolan held a reception for Catholic University alumni in his residence.

The cardinal reminded the nearly 800 guests that, as cohost of the 2001 event, Cardinal Egan set a record for the most raised, a total of $2 million.

Dolan was delighted to then announce a new record of $2.1 million had been set by this gala. Since its inauguration, the American cardinals dinners have raised more than $32.5 million to support scholarships for Catholic University students.

At the conclusion of the gala, Cardinal Egan delivered the final benediction and St. Louis Archbishop Robert J. Carlson, a Catholic University alumnus and member of the Catholic University board, stated that the 2015 American Cardinals Dinner would be held April 24 in his archdiocese. St. Louis Archbishop Carlson reminded the guests that St. Louis is the home of a group of cardinals of a different sort. As an encouragement to meet him in St. Louis next year, on their departure everyone assembled received a signature Stan Musial Harmonica, which was produced as a memento of the St. Louis Cardinals Hall of Famer, famous for his harmonica rendition of the "Meet Me in St. Louis" classic.

The 26th American Cardinals Dinner, St. Louis

April 24, 2015

The 26th American Cardinals Dinner was held was held Friday, April 24, 2015, at the Ritz-Carlton, St. Louis, hosted by Most Rev. Robert J. Carlson, archbishop of St. Louis, and John Garvey, president of The Catholic University of America. It was the first time St. Louis was the site of the dinner, which rotate to a different city each year, becoming the 16th United States city to host one of these annual events. A 4:30 p.m. Mass was held prior to the dinner at the famed Cathedral Basilica of Saint Louis, one of the most beautiful churches in America, concelebrated by six cardinals, with Archbishop Carlson, who received a Licentiate in Canon Law from Catholic University, the principal celebrant and homilist. Visiting bishops and clergy also were concelebrants. At both the Mass and the dinner a moment of silence was held in memory of two cardinals who had passed away since the

last dinner. Cardinal Edward M. Egan, retired archbishop of New York, died in early March and Cardinal Francis E, George, O.M.I., archbishop of Chicago, passed away on April 17. Both were very supportive of The Catholic University of America and of the American Cardinals dinners.

"We are honored that St. Louis has been chosen as the location for the 2015 American Cardinals Dinner," said Archbishop Carlson. "St. Louis is not only a great baseball Cardinals town, but as the 'Rome of the West' it boasts a proud Catholic history, including many cardinals who have called St. Louis home."

Charles and Shirley Drury were cochairs of the black-tie gala and were honored with the Archbishop's Appreciation Award, acknowledging their consistent generosity to and involvement with the Archdiocese of St. Louis and a variety of other Catholic causes. Special acknowledgement and appreciation was made to the Drury's and the other principal benefactors of the event, Richard D. Banziger, the Knights of Columbus, and the Archdiocese of St. Louis. Also providing

The 26th American Cardinals Dinner
Left to right seated: Cardinal McCarrick, Cardinal DiNardo, Cardinal Dolan, and Cardinal Rigali. Standing left to right: Cardinal Wuerl, President Garvey, Archbishop Carlson, and Cardinal O'Malley.

President John Garvey extending his appreciation to those attending the dinner for their generosity in providing scholarship assistance to Catholic University students.

significant support were Dr. Anthony R. Tersigni, Jim and Jeanne Moye, Mr. and Mrs. Donald L. Ross, and Dr. Enrique Segura. Several Catholic University students who were receiving scholarship assistance expressed their sincere appreciation for what the scholarship support means to them.

The St. Louis dinner raised more than $1.1 million for scholarships to benefit Catholic University students. Six American cardinals were the honored guests, all of whom are graduates of CUA: Cardinal Seán O'Malley, O.F.M. Cap., archbishop of Boston; Cardinal Daniel N. DiNardo, archbishop of Galveston-Houston; Cardinal Donald W. Wuerl, archbishop of Washington and chancellor of the university; Cardinal Timothy M. Dolan, archbishop of New York and a native of St. Louis; Cardinal Theodore E. McCarrick, archbishop emeritus of Washington; and Cardinal Justin F. Rigali, archbishop emeritus of Philadelphia and a former archbishop of St. Louis.

The magnificent Cathedral Basilica of St. Louis, one of the most beautiful cathedrals in the Unites States, site of The 26th American Cardinals Dinner.

Archbishop Robert J. Carlson of St. Louis presenting the Archbishop's Appreciation Award to Shirley and Charles Drury, with President John Garvey looking on.

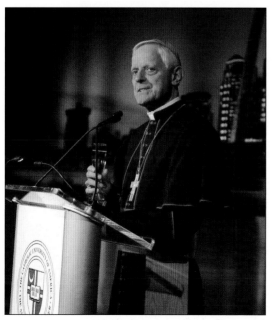

Cardinal Donald W. Wuerl, chancellor of Catholic University, addressing the assembled guests.

In expressing his appreciation to the host archbishop, President John Garvey said,

I am very grateful to Archbishop Carlson for graciously agreeing to host this scholarship fund-raiser in St. Louis for our students. As the national university of the Catholic Church, we have students and alumni from all 50 U.S. states. We host this dinner in a different city each year, to make ourselves better known and to emphasize that we exist to serve Catholics in the American heartland, on both coasts, and everywhere in between.

The previous event, which commemorated the Silver Anniversary of the initiation of these dinners in 1987, was held in New York City. Past dinners have been held in such cities as Phoenix, Atlanta, Houston, Boston, Las Vegas, Miami, Minneapolis-St. Paul, San Francisco, Washington, D.C., and Chicago.

The concelebrants at the Mass in the Cathedral Basilica of St. Louis held the afternoon of the gala event.

Cardinal Edward Egan
Archbishop of New York

Cardinal Edward M. Egan Dies at Age 82

The retired archbishop of New York, Cardinal Edward M. Egan, died suddenly of cardiac arrest on March 5, 2015, in his residence. Egan was the 12th bishop, ninth archbishop, and seventh cardinal of New York. In February 2009, he was the first to retire, all others dying in office. He was a native of Chicago and spent 23 years in the Vatican, becoming a judge of the Sacred Roman Rota. He had been a priest for 57 years, a bishop for 29 years, and a cardinal for 14 years. Cardinal Egan attended eight American cardinals dinners and hosted one, in New York, in 2001.

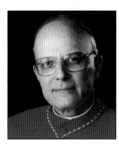

Cardinal Francis George
Archbishop of Chicago
M.A. 1965

Cardinal Francis E. George, O.M.I., Dies at Age 78

The retired archbishop of Chicago, Cardinal Francis E. George, O.M.I., passed away on April 17, 2015, one week before The 26th American Cardinals Dinner, after battling cancer for almost 10 years. George attended a dozen American cardinals dinners and hosted two in Chicago, in 2000 and 2012. He earned a master's degree at The Catholic University of America in 1965. Cardinal George was the eighth archbishop of Chicago and, in November 2014, the first to retire. He was the first native Chicagoan to lead the archdiocese. He had been a priest for 51 years, a bishop for 24 years, and a cardinal for 17 years.

Cardinal William Baum
Archbishop of
Washington
CUA Chancellor
1973–1980

Cardinal William Wakefield Baum Dies at Age 88

Cardinal William Wakefield Baum died after a long illness on July 23, 2015, in Washington, D.C. He was a cardinal for 39 years, the longest tenure of any United States cardinal in history, surpassing the previous record of 34 years by Cardinal James Gibbons, archbishop of Baltimore and first chancellor of The Catholic University of America from 1887 to 1921. Baum was archbishop of Washington and chancellor of Catholic University from 1973 to 1980, when he was transferred to the Vatican Curia in Rome. Cardinal Baum spent the remainder of his priestly life in service to the Church at the Vatican, but was able to attend two American cardinals dinners, in 1993 and 2006. He had been a priest for 64 years and a bishop for 45 years.

Afterword

The intimate tie between the cardinals of the United States and The Catholic University of America has been ongoing since the inception of the university and was strengthened during the quarter century of American cardinals dinners. The cardinals have clearly exhibited their support and encouragement by their personal attendance at these events, year after year.

Including Cardinal Timothy Dolan, who cohosted The 25th American Cardinals Dinner, 14 cardinals who have led residential sees in the United States have cohosted dinners on behalf of the university: Two each by cardinals Hickey, Bevilacqua, George, and Law. One each by cardinals Bernardin, O'Connor, Mahony, Keeler, Maida, McCarrick, Egan, O'Malley, DiNardo, Wuerl, and Dolan.

In addition, five other United States cardinals have attended American cardinals dinners at various times over this 26-year period: Cardinal Krol, Cardinal Baum, Cardinal Szoka, Cardinal Dulles, and Cardinal Rigali. Among other cardinals who have attended the dinners are Cardinal Laghi, former apostolic nuncio to the United States, and Cardinal Daly, archbishop of Armagh and Primate of All Ireland.

A review of the cities serving as sites of these dinners is evidence that The Catholic University of America is the national Catholic university. Between 1989 and 2015, American cardinals dinners have been held in 16 different cities in 15 states and the District of Columbia. Dinners have been held in Washington four times; in Chicago, Boston, and New York three times each; in Philadelphia twice; and in St. Louis, Los Angeles, San Francisco, Detroit, Baltimore, St. Paul, Miami, Las Vegas, Houston, Atlanta, and Scottsdale once.

Each of the five archbishops who have represented the Vatican in the United States during this period as apostolic nuncio has been present each year. In turn, each nuncio addressed the gathering to convey the greetings of the Holy Father. The apostolic nuncios and their tenure in the United States: Pio Laghi, February 10, 1980, to April 6, 1990; Agostino Cacciavillan, June 13, 1990, to November 5, 1998; Gabriel Montalvo, December 7, 1998, to December 17, 2005; Pietro Sambi, December 17, 2005, to July 27, 2011; and Carlo Maria Viganò, beginning in October 2011.

The four presidents of The Catholic University of America who have cohosted dinners— Rev. William J. Byron, S.J.; Brother Patrick Ellis, F.S.C.; Very Rev. David M. O'Connell, C.M.; and John Garvey—have found these events to be enormously rewarding to the university from a variety of viewpoints, not the least of which is the fact that the university scholarship fund realized more than $33.5 million.

EPILOGUE

September of 2015 saw the return of the United States cardinals to the nation's capital to greet Pope Francis upon his arrival on the 22nd when he began his first papal visit to the Unites States. The Holy Father is the third pontiff to visit the campus of The Catholic University of America.

The initial event leading to the Pope's visit to the United States was to participate at the World Meeting of Families held in Philadelphia on the Sept. 26 and 27. In Washington, Pope Francis met with President Barack Obama at the White House. On September 23, the Holy Father celebrated an outdoor Mass of canonization of Junípero Serra on the East Portico of the Basilica Shrine of the Immaculate Conception, with the congregation gathered on the lawn of the Catholic University

Large banners were displayed throughout the campus welcoming the Holy Father.

Pope Francis greeting the cheering crowd from his popemobile.

campus. The next day he addressed a Joint Session of the United States Congress. From Washington, the Holy Father visited New York City, where he addressed the United Nations General Assembly, attended a multireligious service at the 9/11 Memorial at the World Trade Center, held a vespers service at St. Patrick's Cathedral, and celebrated Mass at Madison Square Garden. He then went on to the meeting in Philadelphia, where he also celebrated a closing Mass outside the Philadelphia Art Museum.

Catholic University is the only educational institution in the United States having a Holy Father present on its campus more than once. Three have visited: Pope John Paul II in 1979, Pope Benedict XIV in 2008, and Pope Francis in 2015.

Cardinal Donald W. Wuerl, archbishop of Washington and chancellor of Catholic University greeting the Holy Father.

Pope Francis celebrated a Mass of canonization of Franciscan Father Junipero Serra.

In September 2015, Pope Francis became the third pontiff to visit at Catholic University. Pope John Paul II delivered an address at CUA in 1979 and Pope Benedict XVI in 2008.

A view of a portion of the thousands who attended the papal Mass. McMahon Hall is in the background.

Pope Francis, September 2015, at Catholic University.

CARDINALS OF THE UNITED STATES

———————

Following is a list of the 52 United States Cardinals, in the order they were named, as of Founders Day, April 10, 2016, the 129th anniversary of the creation of The Catholic University of America. Since the university was established by Pope Leo XIII in 1887, all resident cardinals of the United States have become members of its Board of Trustees.

Cardinal John Mc Closkey	Cardinal Timothy Manning
Cardinal James Gibbons	Cardinal Humberto S. Medeiros
Cardinal John M. Farley	Cardinal William W. Baum
Cardinal William H. O'Connell	Cardinal Joseph L. Bernardin
Cardinal Dennis J. Dougherty	Cardinal Bernard F. Law
Cardinal George W. Mundelein	Cardinal John J. O'Connor
Cardinal Patrick J. Hayes	Cardinal James A. Hickey
Cardinal John J. Glennon	Cardinal Edmund C. Szoka
Cardinal Edward A. Mooney	Cardinal Roger M. Mahony
Cardinal Samuel A. Stritch	Cardinal Anthony J. Bevilacqua
Cardinal Francis J. Spellman	Cardinal William H. Keeler
Cardinal J. Francis McIntyre	Cardinal Adam J. Maida
Cardinal Richard J. Cushing	Cardinal J. Francis Stafford
Cardinal John F. O'Hara, C.S.C.	Cardinal Francis E. George, O.M.I.
Cardinal Aloysius J. Muench	Cardinal Theodore E. McCarrick
Cardinal Albert G. Meyer	Cardinal Edward M. Egan
Cardinal Joseph Elmer Ritter	Cardinal Avery Dulles, S.J.
Cardinal Lawrence J. Shehan	Cardinal Justin F. Rigali
Cardinal Patrick A. O'Boyle	Cardinal William J. Levada
Cardinal John J. Krol	Cardinal Seán P. O'Malley, O.F.M. Cap
Cardinal John P. Cody	Cardinal John P. Foley
Cardinal Francis J. Brennan	Cardinal Daniel N. DiNardo
Cardinal John F. Dearden	Cardinal Raymond Leo Burke
Cardinal John J. Carberry	Cardinal Donald W. Wuerl
Cardinal Terence J. Cooke	Cardinal Edwin F. O'Brien
Cardinal John J. Wright	Cardinal Timothy M. Dolan

ACKNOWLEDGMENTS

A sincere debt of gratitude is extended to the dozens of people at The Catholic University of America who provided assistance in the preparation of this work. From the outset, I received the approval, encouragement, and complete assistance of the president, John Garvey, and his chief of staff, Frank Persico, as well as their associates in the president's office, including Joy Zang, Bill Jonas, and Suzanne McCarthy. I had the privilege of discussing the American cardinals dinners with three former Catholic University presidents, who were generous with their commentary, Rev. William J. Byron, S.J, Brother Patrick Ellis, F.S.C. (several weeks before he passed away), and Bishop David M. O'Connell, C.M.

Thanks are extended to Frank Persico and Bill Jonas for their review and early assessment of preliminary drafts. The CUA Office of Public Affairs, led by Victor Nakas, was particularly kind in providing information and by encouraging his staff to assist in every way. A special note of appreciation to Carol Casey, who, early on, dug out scores of old CUA magazines and press releases on dinners, which provided invaluable source material, and to Donna Hobson, who never failed to respond to a request. A key element to this book was the editing of the completed manuscript by Carol Casey. I don't think it is possible to find anyone who can perform this task better than Carol. Her line-by-line editing was exceptional and her ability to reconstruct sentences and paragraphs, while maintaining the essence of the copy, was extraordinary.

Valuable archival assistance was provided by the entire staff of the American Catholic History Research Center and University Archives at The Catholic University of America led by curator and University Archivist Tim Meagher. Particularly helpful were John Shepherd, Jane Stoeffler, and Shane MacDonald. My appreciation to the Office of Public Affairs and the CUA Archives for providing all of the pictures appearing in this book, with a few exceptions, which are noted where the photo appears.

It has been a joy working at and for The Catholic University of America, an outstanding educational institution which I, like all Catholics in the nation, proudly can call "my university."

Martin J. Moran

For
Kate Janiki
SK

For
Ross
AM

First published 2001 by AMO Productions,
106 Rutland Grove, Dublin 12, Ireland.
Tel: +353 1 454 5182 Fax: +353 1 454 5182
E-mail: amo@iol.ie
Website: www.amoproductions.com

ISBN 0-9540995-0-8

Written and created by **AnnMarie O'Grady**

Illustrated by **Stella Kearns**

Photography by **Gerry Smith**

Design and Cover by **Crackerjack Design**

Printed by **Colourbooks Ltd**

AMO Productions in association with

Little Bits of Ireland

Written and created by
AnnMarie O'Grady

Illustrated by
Stella Kearns

Contents

Ireland - An Introduction

Ireland is a small country in Europe. It is surrounded by the sea. The following is a fun map of Ireland which shows you some of the places that you might visit.

Co. Donegal

Co. Antrim

ULSTER

Newgrange

Co. Meath

Co. Galway

LEINSTER

Co. Dublin

CONNAUGHT

Glendalough
Co. Wicklow

Co. Wexford

MUNSTER
Co. Waterford

Co. Kerry

Co. Cork

| Dublin | Dublin is the capital city of Ireland. |

| Wicklow | Later we can hear the story of King O'Toole and St. Kevin of Glendalough in Wicklow |

| Galway | Galway is famous for its green fields surrounded by dry stone walls. Sometimes if we are driving in Galway we can see sheep on the road! |

| Meath | Newgrange is in Co. Meath. Later we can read about this famous place in Ireland, and make our own simple Newgrange ornaments.
We will also be making a castle very similar to Trim Castle in Co. Meath on page 46 |

| Kerry | We can see Gallarus Oratory on p.23 and the beehive huts on p. 22 in Co. Kerry. It is known for its beautiful countryside. |

There are many places to visit which can be seen on our map such as Cork, Wexford, Waterford, Donegal, Limerick and many more.

Welcome

Ireland is a very special country rich in art, tradition and folklore. There are many Saints and Scholars lives that we can read about in our history books. The Book of Kells is one of the most famous treasures in Europe, this can be seen in Trinity College, Dublin. There are unmatched, unique manuscripts, chalices and jewellery made thousands of years ago in Ireland which can now be seen in museums.

The landscape is covered with beautiful preserved churches, castles, dolmens and high crosses all of which were built many years ago. There is also breathtaking scenery of green fields, mountains and flowing rivers. This makes Ireland an exciting country to visit. People from many countries come to see the enchanting countryside and experience our history associated with this little country.

Let's discover some of our history and recreate our "heritage" in a fun way.

Farming in Ireland

Ireland has a mild climate which means there is plenty of rain. This makes the grass grow and the fields green. It is therefore a very good place for animals to graze in the fields. This is why farming is very important in Ireland. If we drive through the countryside we can see many types of farm animals eating the green grass of the fields.

Although sheep and pigs are raised on farms, cattle are more popular. Ireland's rich grass is grazed by over two million cows.

If you read on, you can make your own fun farm animal folders.

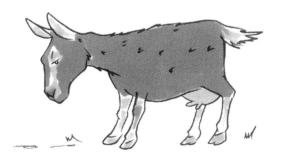

Make Your Own Fun Farm Animal Folders

You Will Need

* **A4 coloured card**
* **Some furry material**
* **Needle and thread**
* **Small piece of card**
* **Pegs**
* **Double-sided sticky tape or glue**
* **Animal eyes, nose**
* **2 green pipe cleaners**
* **1 black pipe cleaner**
* **Scissors**

1 Firstly, get a peg and glue it onto the top middle, of the A4 coloured card. Allow to dry.

COW

2 Cut the following shape with the furry material.

2.

3 To make the ears, cut the following arch shape.

3.

4 Sew the top edge. Tie a knot and pull the thread to gather the edge. Do this twice for both ears. Get a grown-up to help you with the sewing.

5 Sew this piece onto the top right and left hand corner, to create ears on the face.

6 Make a hole and attach his eyes.

The craft eyes usually come with backing to secure, if not then use a good glue to secure.

7 Attach the nose in a similar fashion.

8 Use the black pipe cleaner to make a smiley mouth. The shamrock is made by first a cross shape and then three love heart leaf shapes which can be twisted around the smiley mouth.

Then simply sew this onto the cow face.

9 Glue the cow shape onto card. It can then be attached to the peg with double sided sticky tape.

Well done! You have made a fun farm animal folder.

If you would like to make a sheep folder then read on!!

SHEEP

To make the sheep's face, follow steps 1-5 on how to make the cow's face, but shape of his face is slightly different.

1 He is made with black fur and a white piece of fur is sewn to the top of the head. Attach his eyes with glue.

3 Cut a hole in a straight line where his teeth will be placed.

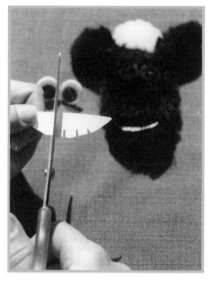

4 You can make the teeth by cutting white card from the following shape.

5 To hide the teeth, place them under the black fur and sew or glue them in place. The teeth give the sheep a fun look.

6 Glue him onto card. It can then be attached to the peg with double sided sticky tape.

Well done. You have now made your own fun folders that you can write notes to your family or friends.

Ancient Monuments - Newgrange

Newgrange in Co. Meath is a passage grave or tomb. It is thought to have been built thousands of years ago, around 2000 BC. People now believe that the mounds were used by our ancestors to worship or as a burial ground. It is known as a megalithic tomb because it is built of big stones. Megalithic comes from the Greek language. The Greek word 'megas' means great and 'lithos' means stone.

These huge stones were impossible to carry by one person alone. They needed a group of people to help carry the stones. They were first sailed up the River Boyne and then transported on a group of logs. The heavy stone would have been pulled by some of the tomb builders. The others would move the logs to keep the stone moving. The last log would be placed at the front while the logs were still moving. The remaining last log would be placed at the front and so forth. The other men would keep pulling the huge stone with rope. This was the only way to carry the heavy stones.

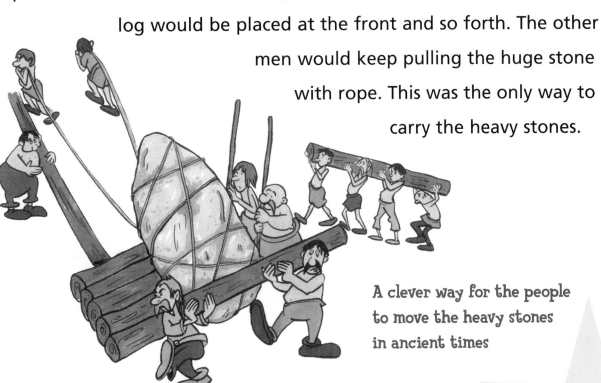

A clever way for the people to move the heavy stones in ancient times

Newgrange has a famous stone marking the entrance to a hidden chamber deep inside the mound. The entrance stone is decorated with carvings of spirals, diamonds and V- shapes. These designs probably had some relevant meaning to the people who built Newgrange all those years ago.

Decorated entrance stone, Newgrange, Co Meath

Today we can only guess the meanings of the beautiful shapes. The design of this stone is still very famous today. It can be seen on jewellery, in books and on writing paper.

Dry Stone Walls

Another thing to notice about Newgrange is that the walls and roof were built without the use of cement. This is therefore an example of a dry stone wall. They placed the stones in a very clever way, so that any rain seeping through the roof was drained away. This meant that the inside central chamber was kept completely dry.

There is a small opening over the entrance covered by a decorated stone. Through this gap the first rays of morning sun of the winter solstice (December 21st- 23rd) shine through. This lights up the inside chamber. It is very exciting for explorers to experience the suns first rays in this ancient tomb as it happens on only one day of the year. For a few brief moments we can share this special creation with our ancestors - a clever people.

Dry stone walls are still a landmark in Ireland and can be seen scattered around the Irish countryside.

Make your own Newgrange ornaments

You Will Need

* 2 coloured pipe cleaners

It should stand
up like this...

The following design is taken from the entrance stone at Newgrange.

1 Fold the pipe cleaners into the following cross shape.

2 Take the first line to the left of the cross and twist in the following spiral shape.

3 Skip the lower line and move on to the right hand line. Twist this into a similar spiral shape.

4 Now, pull the top line slightly to the right and then twist into a spiral shape just like the others. It should now look like this.

5 Now all you have to do is fold the lower line back so as the three spiral shapes are at the front and can lean on the back line of the pipe cleaner which is used as a support for your ornament.

The Dolmen

A dolmen is another type of megalithic tomb. It is different to Newgrange. It is called a portal tomb. It is made up of three standing stones, covered by a huge capstone. The capstone covers the burial chamber.

It looks like a huge stone table!

When building the dolmen the people had to be very skilled and careful because the capstones were so heavy. For example, the one at Brownes Hill in Co. Carlow weighs 100 tons. This huge capstone is the largest in Europe. Imagine trying to lift that weight and then put it on on three standing stones!

Countrymen invented some colourful names for the dolmens. They called them 'Giant's Grave's' or sometimes 'Druid's altars'. Lastly some country people called them Diarmuid and Grainne's bed after the famous Irish legend story. The people regard them with respect and even superstition.

There are examples of ancient dolmens scattered all over Ireland especially in Leinster and Ulster. Can you see where this is on the map on Page 6.

Make your own Papier Mache Dolmen

1 For the legs of the dolmen, cut the cardboard into three long rectangular shapes, two equal size and one slightly wider.

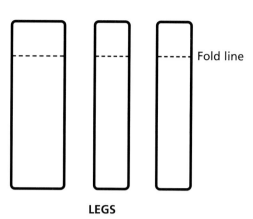

LEGS

Fold line

2 The legs will need to fit through the capstone. We need one thick piece of card that is big enough to fold into the shape of the capstone.

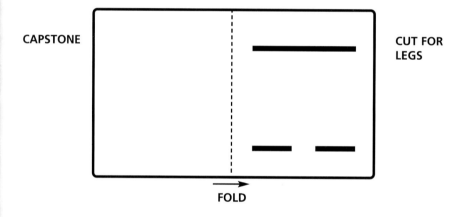

CAPSTONE

CUT FOR LEGS

FOLD

3 Draw a line in the middle where the fold will occur.

4 Now draw three lines where your legs will fit. Cut the three lines where the legs will fit through.

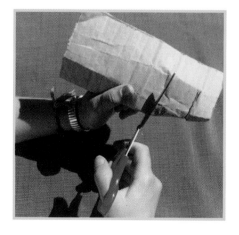

5 Place the three legs through the slots. Sellotape them to secure.

6 When this is done fold the top capstone and Sellotape to secure.

7 Mix wallpaper paste and water until you have a smooth paste.

8 You may now cover the shape with glue and newspaper until the entire surface is covered to resemble rough stone. Allow to dry. This method is known as layered papier-mache.

9 When it is dry you can paint it grey which is like a stone colour. You can place some silver on it to make it shine. If you would like to make it look more like stone you can use some silver and white paint and spray this on with an old toothbrush and a ruler. Put a little paint on the old toothbrush and spray your Dolmen by flicking the toothbrush against the ruler.

It should look like this...

Well done. You have now made your own dolmen, a striking feature of the Irish countryside.

Ogham Stones

Scattered around the country are unusual standing stones with what looks like teethmarks at the side of the stone. This is called ogham script. It is the earliest form of Irish writing. It was an adaptation of the latin alphabet used by Irish poets or learned men.

Explanations of ogham can still be found in manuscripts down to recent times. Our folklore tells us that this writing had a magical significance.

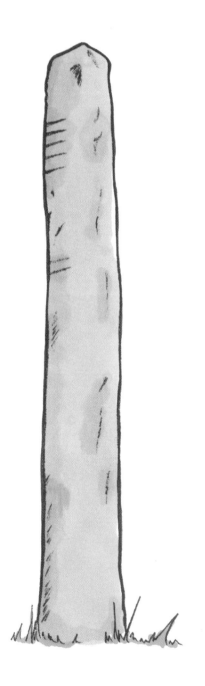

You can make an ogham stone using card and plain layered papier mache similar to the method used when making the dolmen on the previous page. You can use a dark colour to mark the lettering at the side of the stone!!

Were they ancient signposts?

Stone Circles, Standing Stones

Stone circles are associated with the bronze age in Ireland. They generally consist of a ring of five or more standing stones. Inside this man made circle is plain, flat ground. It is unclear as to why these stone circles exist. Some people believe that these stones are linked with the sun and have links with events in the solar calendar.

One story from a Co. Wicklow Stone Circle, says that the Lord cast seven dancers to stone who were dancing in a circle. A standing stone nearby is said to be the piper who was the musician who provided music for the dancers. It is still known as the piper's stone.

The circles were thought to exist in the Iron Age where the centre area was used as a burial ground.

Standing Stone

A standing stone is a rough stone pillar set in the ground. This is the simplest and most common monument in Ireland. They were built many years ago and mark important sites, boundaries or graves. There are legends associated with some of them.

Beehive huts

These are not, as the name suggests, little huts where the bees lived!
They were huts that were shaped very like a beehive. Off the coast of
Co. Kerry there is an island called Skellig Michael, made of a huge
jagged rock. The islanders long ago carved a flight of stairs up the rock
and this leads to the remains of a huge monastic settlement. This is
where some of the Christian monks lived long ago, on a very remote
location in Ireland.

On this island we can see some beehive huts or monk's cells. These
unusual homes are round outside and square inside. They have flat
headed doorways, paved floors and cupboards made from stones. They
are still as weatherproof as the day they were built, over 1000 years ago.

There are some other beehive huts which can be spotted in remote
parts of Co. Kerry.

Gallarus Oratory

Gallarus oratory is on the side of a hill in Dingle in Co. Kerry. It was once part of a small monastery. It is built with stone where once again no cement was used. It is an another excellent example of dry stone walling. It is amazing to think that the unusual oratory, built with old stones and using old techniques, still stands today in perfect condition. Does it make you wonder how Irish people lived a long time ago?

Gallarus Oratory is shaped like an upturned boat. It has a small, narrow doorway with a tiny round window opposite it. Its construction was very similar to that at Newgrange, however the Gallarus Oratory is much smaller.

Crannog - an ancient Irish dwelling

A Crannog is a man-made island, built up by laying down stones in shallow water. The stones are then covered by brush wood. The name is derived from the gaelic word 'crann' which means tree. The wood is then covered by earth on which houses are built. The houses were very simple dwelling places for people long ago.

You can see an example of a reconstructed crannog in Craggaunowen, Co. Clare.

Reconstructed Crannog, Craggaunowen, Co.Clare.

Saints in Ireland

Saint Brendan was known for his love of adventure and travel. He built a boat called a 'curragh'. It is believed that he sailed to America thousands of years ago.

Saint Brigid is known for her generous, kind nature. She has a special cross that we make on February 1st, her feast day.

Saint Ciaran founded a monastery in Clonmacnoise in 544 which we will read about on page 33. He only enjoyed his monastery for a short time as he died of the plague shortly after it was built.

Saint Patrick is the patron saint of Ireland. He is thought to have brought the Christian faith to Ireland. His feast day is on March 17th.

There are many other Saints in Ireland known for their holy work and kindness during their lives.

The Story of Saint Patrick in poetic verse

A long time ago in Ireland
from Britain where he came,
was born to us a special child
and Patrick was his name.

When he was only 16 years
he was seized and made a slave,
upon the hills of Ireland
his life was sad and grave.

He was left to herd the cattle
and left to mind the sheep,
and cold beneath the starry night
is where he had to sleep.

But clever Patrick ran away
and took a brave man's trip,
went all the way to the coast side
and there he found a ship.

At last he was at home again
his parents thrilled to see,
their son returned so safe and well
and happy as could be.

One night then Patrick had a dream
to return to Ireland,
he prayed for help along the way
and a journey soon was planned.

He went to France became a Priest
studied Christianity,
and then returned to Ireland
to set the nation free

He told the people of one God
oft hard to understand,
but his words of power swept right through
and all across the land.

He built Churches where he travelled
where people came to pray,
and converted many people
each and everyday.

And when he died his legend lived
in a land so green and quaint,
they gave to him a special day
and is now our patron Saint

So now on March 17th
is a very special date,
marks the legend of Saint Patrick
we all must celebrate.

With music, song and wearing green
put a smile upon your face,
because it says to us that Ireland
is a very special place.

Churches & Monasteries

With the coming of Saint Patrick people needed somewhere to pray. A lot of people started to devote their time to God and prayer. Some people tried to keep the message of Saint Patrick alive after he died.

Holy people spent their time writing manuscripts with the word of the gospel in Latin. These people were known as monks. They spent each day creating beautiful works of art. They led simple lives devoted to God and learning. Some founded monasteries and became saints in their own right.

We can see some of the early churches were simple places beside the sea or rivers. Gallarus is thought to be one of the first Churches in Ireland. (See page 23)

Clonmacnoise

Clonmacnoise is an example of a monastery founded by a river. It is situated by the River Shannon, the longest river in Ireland. It was founded by St. Ciaran and dates back to 544 AD. It has the beautiful remains of a large monastic settlement.

St Ciaran had a special cow called Dun Cow. It was said that this one cow gave enough milk for everyone in the monastery!

If you ever go to Clonmacnoise you must visit what is now known as the Whispering Arch.

It was made so that people with leprosy could make their confessions when they were sick. They stood at one side of the arch and would whisper into the archway. The monk could hear the confession at the other side of the archway.

Churches built in the twelfth century were known as Romanesque. They contained elaborate rounded decorated archways and beautifully shaped windows.

Cathedrals were even more detailed. Look at this entrance at Clonfert Co. Galway.

The entrance of Clonfert Cathedral

Christchurch Cathedral

Christchurch is Dublin's oldest surviving stone masterpiece. It stands out in Ireland as one of the finest churches and largest parish churches of the middle ages. It was the centre of the old Norsemen. It reflects the sculptural style of the West of England, it has coloured line impressed floor tiles and beautiful stained glass windows.

Noah

Joshua's Vision

The baptism of the eunuch

Here is an example of some of the stained glass windows in Christchurch Cathedral

Make your own Church
with stained glass windows

You Will Need

* **2 cardboard boxes**

  1 large (for church)

  1 small (for steeple)

* **grey & bronze, white & silver paint**

* **strips of purple paper**

* **White card (large for roof)**

* **tracing paper**

* **colouring markers**

* **black felt tip pen**

* **2 grey pipecleaners**

* **Sellotape**

* **Scissors**

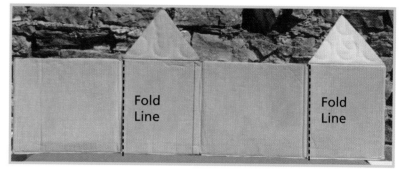

Fold Line   Fold Line

1 Cut out the following shape with the large box.

2 On the following page are the window shapes. Trace outline onto cardboard and cut out. Now use the shape as a stencil and mark it out where you are placing your windows.

We put the windows on all sides of the box.   Door

36

3 Now use a scissors to cut out where the windows will be.

4 Now it is ready to paint. If the grey paint will not go on directly you will have to use newspaper and paste layers all around the church (see Page 19, Instruction No. 7 & 8). Allow to dry and then paint it grey, you can use the toothbrush seen on page 48 (fig 6, introduction no. 7) for the effect of rough stone finish. Paint the door any colour you like. We chose bronze.

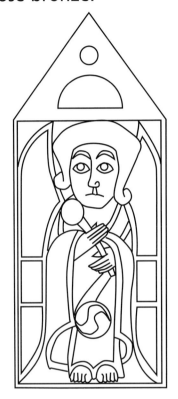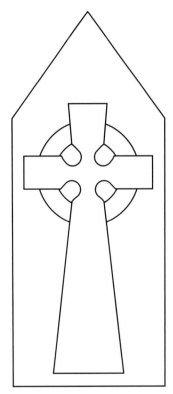

5 Use the tracing paper and trace the following designs for the windows with a black felt pen. Colour them in bright, fun colours. You will need one for each window. We have 8 windows of this shape in our church. You will need to trace and colour them 8 times. There are also two diamond shapes above the side windows.

6 When the church walls are dry, fix the tracing paper windows behind on the inside of the church in the spaces you have provided.

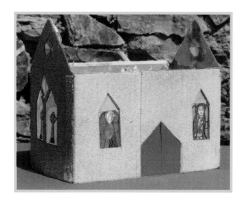

7 Now fold the box back to stand upright. Sellotape to secure.

Cut out a roof in white card that fills the space left for the roof. Now glue the strips of purple paper on this to make a roof. If you are going to make a steeple you will need to leave a gap in the roof to allow the steeple to be attached.

Making the Steeple

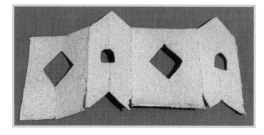 

1 You can also add a steeple onto the roof. You will have to get a smaller lighter box, cut out diamond shapes for the windows. Keep them simple. Paint the steeple in the same way as you did in the main body of the church.

2 You can use the tracing paper to colour in the window shapes.

3 When the windows are attached stand upright and tape together to secure to form a tall rectangle tower.

The roof of the steeple is shaped as shown in *Fig 1*. Complete in a similar way to the church roof.

Fig 1

4 You can make a simple cross and attach that to the steeple roof as shown in *Fig 2*. Ours is simply made with a pipecleaner.

Fig 2

5 Attach the roof onto the steeple with glue or sellotape.

Now it is ready to attach to the main body of the church. Simply place this on the main body of the church and tape to secure from the inside.

There is so much involved in the church that it is a nice group project for a class or a group of friends to make.

If you put a small torch light in it, the windows will illuminate. It is beautiful to see the coloured windows shining in the dark!!!

Well done. You have now made a colourful church that lights up in the dark.

Make your own colourful Window Hangs

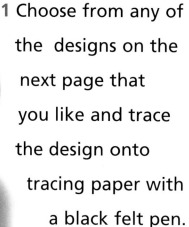

1 Choose from any of the designs on the next page that you like and trace the design onto tracing paper with a black felt pen.

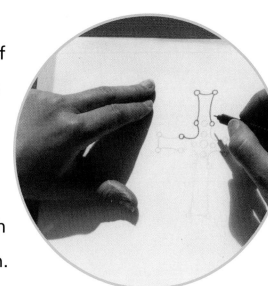

2 Colour the tracing paper designs with brightly coloured markers.

3 Now simply fold a piece of coloured card in two. Fold again and cut any shape you like to form the card frame.

Note, if you like circles, you will only need to cut a semi-circle as when it folds back it will double in size. This will apply to all shapes.

4 Fix the tracing inside the card frame.

Glue around the tracing or use double-sided sticky tape to secure.

You Will Need

* **tracing paper**
* **coloured card**
* **colouring markers**
* **black felt pen**
* **glue or tape**
* **string**
* **double sided sticky tape**
* **Scissors**

5 You can do this as often as you like. If you use a single hole punch to put a hole in the top and the bottom of the window hang you can have a chain of window hangs. It might be fun to make one with your friends.

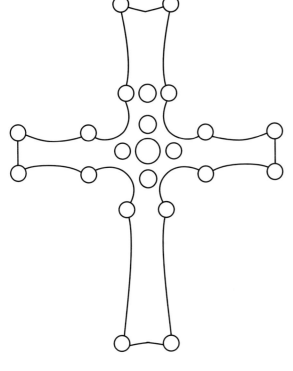

You can make your window hang as long as you like!!

Now it is ready to hang in the window.

41

Make your own Stained Glass Window Candle Holder

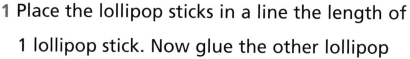

You Will Need

* **lollipop sticks**
* **See through / clear plastic card**
* **glass paints**
* **white spirit**
* **nightlight candles**
* **black outliner for glass paints**
* **Scissors**

1 Place the lollipop sticks in a line the length of 1 lollipop stick. Now glue the other lollipop sticks on top in the alternative direction as shown.

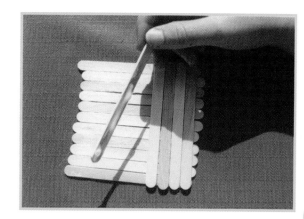

2 At the top of candle holder you will need two rows of eight lollipop sticks glued on top of each other on the flat side.

3 Paint the holder any colour you like.

4 Now cut a strong clear plastic card into a square or arch shape. The width must be the length of a lollipop stick so it will fit in its holder.

5 Use a tube of black outliner for glass paints to trace some of the simple designs on page 41.

Allow to dry.

6 Now paint your design with glass coloured paints. Again allow to dry. You will need to clean your bowls with white spirit. (Ask your parents/teacher to do this).

7 Place the dry plastic card into the space between the top rows of eight lollipop sticks.

Well done. You have now finished.

Now you can get a nightlight to show off your pretty design in the evening time.

Only do this if there is an adult with you.

Castles

The first type of castles were brought to Ireland by the Normans around 1169. They were easy and quick to build. These were known as Motte and Bailey Castles. This type of castle was made up of a steep wooden tower (the Motte) and a wall (the Bailey) surrounding the fortress. They were built with the hope of keeping enemies away.

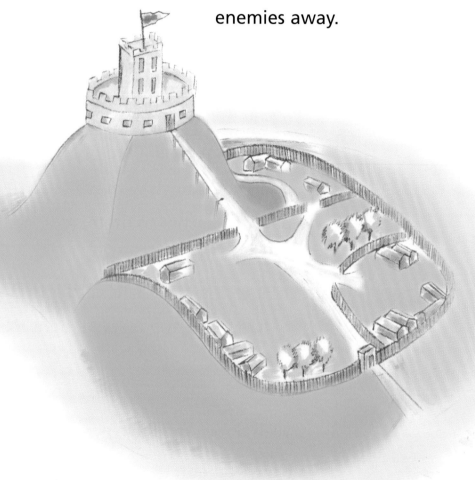

Then
people
started to build
castles out of stone.
These were called Keep and Curtain castles. They were made up of a central rectangular stone tower (the keep) and a surrounding wall (the curtain). These were often protected by a double-towered gate house entrance.

A castle was not a home built like our homes today. It was built to keep enemies out. There were small windows and arrow loops on the lower floors so that the residents could defend/protect themselves if they were attacked by an enemy. The small windows were easy to fire shots from but harder to get shots through. However, these rooms on the lower floors were often dark and cold.

People lived on the higher floors which were safely lit by larger windows. Although castles were built for protection against enemies, most people lived in comfort in them.

The castles sometimes had secret tunnels and rooms so that treasure or riches could be hidden if  the castle was attacked by an enemy. The castle also had murder holes above the entrance and in higher rooms. These were little openings in the floors where an enemy could be shot with arrows in times of danger. Imagine if we had holes in our floors today! Maybe people would think we had mice in our house!

The Normans also had an influence on our castles. This can be seen in castles that had a high rectangular keep with a circular or small round tower at each of the corners.

We can see castles like these in many places in Ireland. Trim Castle is an excellent example of a keep and curtain castle. You can see how striking it is in the picture below. It also had outer ring walls and a gate house.

Trim Castle, Co Meath

Make your own Irish Castle with twin tower gate house

You Will Need

* grey, silver and white paint
* six empty toilet rolls
* a cardboard box
* cardboard sheet
* scissors
* an old tooth brush
* paintbrush
* newspaper, wallpaper paste
* sellotape

1 First we will make the body of the castle. Cut away the folds at the top end of the box.

2 Now we will make the four round turrets. Take the empty toilet roll core and place it on the top corner of the base of the cardboard box. Draw around it with a pencil. Do the same on all four corners. *(See Fig. 1 & 2)*

Fig. 1

Fig. 2

3 Get an adult to cut around these pencil marks with a blade or scissors. They can also cut small holes for windows and an entrance in the empty box, preferably arch shape.

Fig. 3

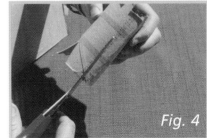
Fig. 4

4 Cut square gaps on one end of the toilet roll. *(See Fig. 3)*

5 Now place a toilet roll in each of the four corners. You may sellotape them on the inside to secure. Make sure the cut tops face upwards to make it look more like castle turrets. Use four toilet rolls, one for each corner of the castle.

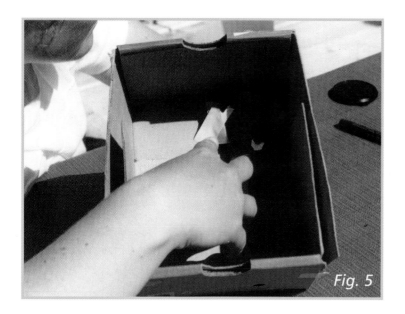
Fig. 5

The remaining two toilet rolls will be used for the twin-towered gate house.

6 Now it is time to get your newspaper and paste ready. Paste a thin layer of newspaper onto the castle.

7 Allow to dry and paint the castle grey. A few coats of paint are advisable. Then you may also use a toothbrush and a lollipop stick to create a stone effect. Place the paint on the toothbrush and flick onto castle. Do the same with white and silver paint. *(See Fig. 6)*

Well done. You have now made your own castle. Now complete the castle by making the twin towered gate house.

Fig. 6

Twin towered gate house

1 To make the surrounding keep walls, get a long strip of cardboard; one that would easily fit around the castle with some room to spare. Fold in two. Sellotape the two edges together. Now paste a thin layer of newspaper around it.

2 Apply a thin layer of newspaper to the remaining two toilet rolls.

3 Allow to dry and apply grey paint and stone effect as you did on the castle.

4 Again, allow to dry and then cut a small gap in the toilet rolls, the height of the wall. Now you can fit the cardboard in this gap as follows. You might need to use a little glue to secure.

5 Paint the same colour as the castle. Place around the main body of the castle.

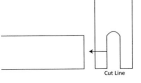

Cut Line

You can add some trees and greenery to create a garden within the grounds of the castle. You might also place some of your own toys or soldiers inside to make it look like an ancient castle. At night time you can put a night light or torch inside the main castle so the windows light up in the dark!! Only do this if there is an adult with you.

Well done. You have now made your own castle and twin towered gate house.

The Viking Invasions

At the end of the eighth century, Ireland suffered many raids and theft by warriors who sailed from the North of Europe. These strangers built big boats and sailed to foreign lands. They became more warlike and they often invaded countries to steal treasure and precious goods. These people were called 'the Vikings'.

Ireland was known as a wealthy country with beautiful treasures made from silver and gold. The monks spent years working on coloured manuscripts and beautiful works of art. The Vikings were merciless. They burned and stole their way across Ireland. They sailed inland on the rivers and invaded monasteries where the monks lived and stole all their work that had taken years to create. It was a very hard time for the Irish.

The Vikings traded goods in Dublin. During recent times the original old city walls and streets were discovered below our modern streets and buildings. An example is Christchurch. The excavators found many ancient goods from that time. These goods can now be seen at the National Museum in Dublin.

The Development of the Irish Round Tower

The monks needed to build something different to protect themselves and their possessions. Something tall so they could see their enemy coming. So they built what was called Round Towers. These towers had four windows at the top facing north, south, east and west.

The Round Tower was also used as a bell house. In peaceful times a monk rang handmade bells to gather the monks from surrounding fields. In Gaelic the tower was called a 'cloigteach' which means bell house.

In times of invasions the monks used the tower to keep themselves and their treasures safe from attack. To get into the tower they climbed a ladder and entered through a doorway which was placed high above the ground. The ladder was then pulled into the tower. This way the Vikings could not get into the tower. If they did, there were more ladders used that went up the tower for three or four storeys high. Each storey had wooden floor and was dimly lit by a small window. The windows on each storey faced different directions. The clever monks had found a way to keep themselves and their treasures safe!

These round towers are solely associated with Ireland. They are very unusual and unique. They can be seen in various places throughout the country, particularly near churches or holy places.

Make your own round tower

You Will Need

* **black and grey paint** (also silver paint if you would like to make it shine a little like we did on the dolmen on page 19)

* **a large piece of white card or watercolour paper**

* **purple card**

* **a stapler**

* **glue**

* **black colouring pencil**

* **sellotape**

* **lollipop sticks**

1 Paint one side of the card grey with a little silver. Allow to dry. *(Fig. 1)*

2 Again make the stone effect from page 48. *(Fig. 6)*

3 Now make the bricks by drawing them in black pencil on your card.

4 Draw in the windows, remember facing all directions in black pencil. *(Fig. 2)*

5 Draw an entrance door above the bottom of the card. *(Fig. 2)*

6 Now make a cylinder shape with this as you see below. Glue or staple this at the back. *(Fig. 3)*

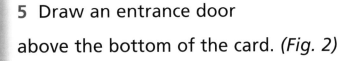

Fig. 1

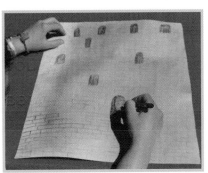

Fig. 2

Fig. 3

The Roof

1 For the roof use the card as with the round tower. Cut a shape like a triangle. With a rounded bottom side. *(Fig. 1)*

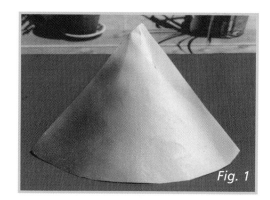
Fig. 1

2 Make the stone affect by spraying on some silver and grey with a toothbrush.

3 Draw on the bricks with pencil. *(Fig. 2)*

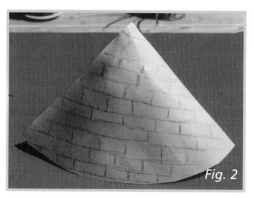
Fig. 2

4 Now make a cone shape and use stapler to secure. Cut away any edges. *(Fig. 3)*

Fig. 3

5 Attach this to the roof with a little bit of glue at the top of the cylinder. If you want to secure it you can put your arm up the cylinder and put sellotape on the inside.

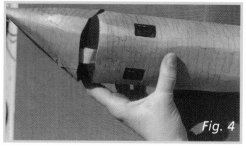
Fig. 4

*Note the ladder is simply made by gluing lollipop sticks together.

Well done you have now made a round tower that the monks used to keep themselves and their treasures safe in ancient times!

Glendalough

Glendalough is a very beautiful place in Ireland with the remains of an old monastic settlement. There is a an old church known as St. Kevin's Church and a round tower surrounded by an atmospheric graveyard and many stone ruins. There are green trees, rolling hills and two lakes. The name comes from the Irish words 'Glen dá logh', which means Glen of two lakes.

Glendalough, Co. Wicklow

There is an old legend folktale associated with Glendalough which tells a lovely story of Saint Kevin and King O'Toole.

Saint Kevin and the story of Glendalough

A long time ago in ancient times in Ireland there was a king called King O' Toole. He came from Glendalough, a very special place. It had peaceful lakes and a waterfall. It was surrounded by beautiful mountains and plenty of green fields.

King O'Toole was a fine, active man. He loved sport, in particular he loved hunting. Everyday the King would get up as early as the sunrise, ride over the beautiful mountains of Glendalough and hunt for deer. He loved life and was a happy man.

As the years passed the King grew old and tired. His legs grew stiff and soon his heart failed him. He no longer could enjoy the pleasure of going hunting. The poor king grew sad. He needed something to bring joy into his life again. So the King got a clever goose.

The goose swam across the lake to catch fish. She flew around the lake and the king was happy once again. The years past, seasons changed and with the slow passing of time, the goose grew tired just as her master before. She could no longer swim or fly and this saddened the king. He became melancholy and his heart was broken.

One morning King O'Toole was walking by the lake. He was thinking of his cruel life when he met a young man. The King looked up and thought he looked like a decent man.

"God save you," said King O'Toole.

"God save you kindly, King O'Toole," said the young man with a smile.

"Hey," the King replied, a little surprised and curious as to how the young man knew him, "how did you come to know my name?"

"Oh, never mind," said the young man. You see, it was Saint Kevin himself, in disguise. "May I ask how your goose is these days, King O'Toole" Saint Kevin inquired.

The King became even more curious as to how the young man knew to inquire about his goose.

"How do you know about my goose?" he asked.

"Never mind," Saint Kevin said again, "I came to know it."

The King was still confused as to how much the young man seemed to know about his life. He felt sure he had not spoken to him before. "Who are you?" he asked in confusion.

"I am an honest man," replied Saint Kevin.

"How do you make your money?" asked the King.

"I make old things as good as new," said Saint Kevin.

"It's a tinker you are," guessed the King.

"No, I am no tinker by trade," said Saint Kevin "and what would you say if I made your goose as good as new?"

Well, the king's eyes nearly jumped out of his head. The thought of having his goose as good as new was something he had never thought possible. With that the King whistled, and down flew the poor goose and waddled slowly up to her master.

The minute Saint Kevin laid eyes on the goose he smiled. "I'll do the job for you," he said with confidence.

"My goodness," said the King with excitement "if you do, I'll say you're the cleverest man in all the seven parishes."

"Aahh, but what will you give me if I do the job for you?" asked Saint Kevin.

"Anything," said the king "I'll give you anything you ask for, isn't that fair?" The King felt happier than he had in a long time just at the thought of his goose being as good as new.

"That sounds fair indeed," said Saint Kevin.

"I'll tell you what. Will you give me all the ground the goose flies over after I make her as good as new?"

"I will," said the king in delight.

"You won't go back on your word," said Saint Kevin.

"It's a deal," said the King, holding out his hand.

"Honor bright," agreed Saint Kevin. Both men shook hands.

With that Saint Kevin spoke to the poor old goose. "Come here" he said gently, "it is I that'll make you a sporting bird. Sign of the cross on you," he whispered and Saint Kevin did as Saints do. He made a sign of the cross on the bird and "whew" the goose took off into the air. She flew like the eagles themselves. She flew by the cliff, over the lake and far beyond the waterfall.

Saint Kevin and the King looked at the goose fly over acres of land.

"What do you have to say to me," said Saint Kevin.

"That there is no art like man," said the King.

"Anything more?" asked St. Kevin.

"That I am forever grateful to you," he grinned.
"Will you give me all the land the goose flew over?" asked Saint Kevin.

"I will," said the King "and you're welcome to it, though its the last acre I have to give."

"You'll keep your word true," asked the saint.

"As true as the sun," promised King O'Toole.

Saint Kevin was pleased with the King. He then introduced himself properly to him.

"I am Saint Kevin, you don't recognise me because I am disguised." The King fell on his knees before him. "It is the great Saint Kevin, I thought I was only talking to a young boy!"

Saint Kevin supported the king after he came into his property. The King was happy to have his goose as good as new as long as he lived.

✳ ✳ ✳ ✳ ✳ ✳ ✳ ✳ ✳

We must remember that this story is an old folktale and may not reflect the exact history of Glendalough. It is true that Saint Kevin founded a monastery and that people from all over the world visit this magical place.

Fairies and Leprechauns

The history of Ireland tells us
many tales of fairies and
mischievous leprechauns. They
were known for their love
of music and games.
The leprechaun was a tiny
shoemaker and was known for
playing all sorts of funny tricks on humans!!

My little leprechaun

One day as I lay dreaming
A friendly little chap,
came up to me all dressed in green
and sat upon my lap.

He looked at me, it made me smile
he took me by surprise,
for though this man was very small
I knew that he was wise.

He told me of a special land,
where precious dreams are made,
and said that we should follow them
and not to be afraid.

For dreams are there to treasure
everywhere we go,
and soon then we shall find our gold
beneath a cool rainbow.

Then off into the distance
I watched him as he went,
I thought about his words to me
and the blessings that he sent.

He was singing down a country road
at once I felt his grace,
I knew this land of special dreams
was a very special place.

The Hawthorn Tree

It was once believed that the fairies lived in hawthorn trees in ancient Ireland. It was thought to be unlucky and unwise to harm the home of a fairy. Some people still believe this to be true today.

Make your own Hawthorn Jewellery Tree

1 The base of the Jewellery tree is made from flour dough mix. You can follow the instructions on p. 73. Leave a gap in the middle of the base to allow five or six pipe cleaners to fit in.

2 The hawthorn jewellery tree is simply made by twisting pipe cleaners together to make the shape of a tree.

3 You can make the tree as big as you like by using plenty of pipe cleaners.

4 Glue the tree into the gap you have left in the base.

5 Paint the base a pretty colour to finish.

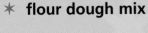
You Will Need

* **black pipe cleaners**
* **flour dough mix**
* **paint**
* **glue**

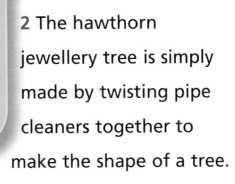

Well done. You can now hang rings on the tree or whatever jewellery you like.

Make your own Leprechaun Puppet

You Will Need

* card
* coloured markers
* string
* 2 sticks
* spray mount or glue
* paper fastners

1 Photocopy the leprechaun on p 68 & 69.

2 Now colour in bright coloured markers.

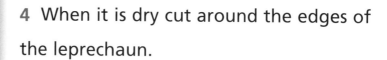

3 Spraymount or glue this onto card.

4 When it is dry cut around the edges of the leprechaun.

5 Cut out his arms and legs.

6 Use a single hole punch to cut holes in the arms and legs and body in the spaces provided.

You can attach these together with a paper fastener.

7 Now to make him dance you will need to make a cross with the sticks.

8 Again use a single hole punch to put holes in his feet, hands and hat.

9 Bring the piece of string from these holes to each corner of the cross.

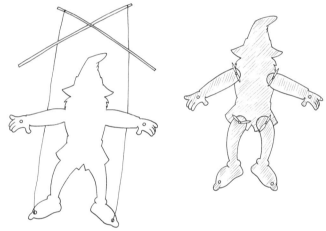

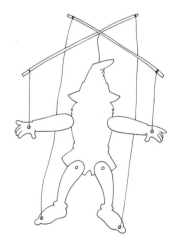

10 Now attach string from his head to his hat.

Well done. Your leprechaun is now ready to dance!!

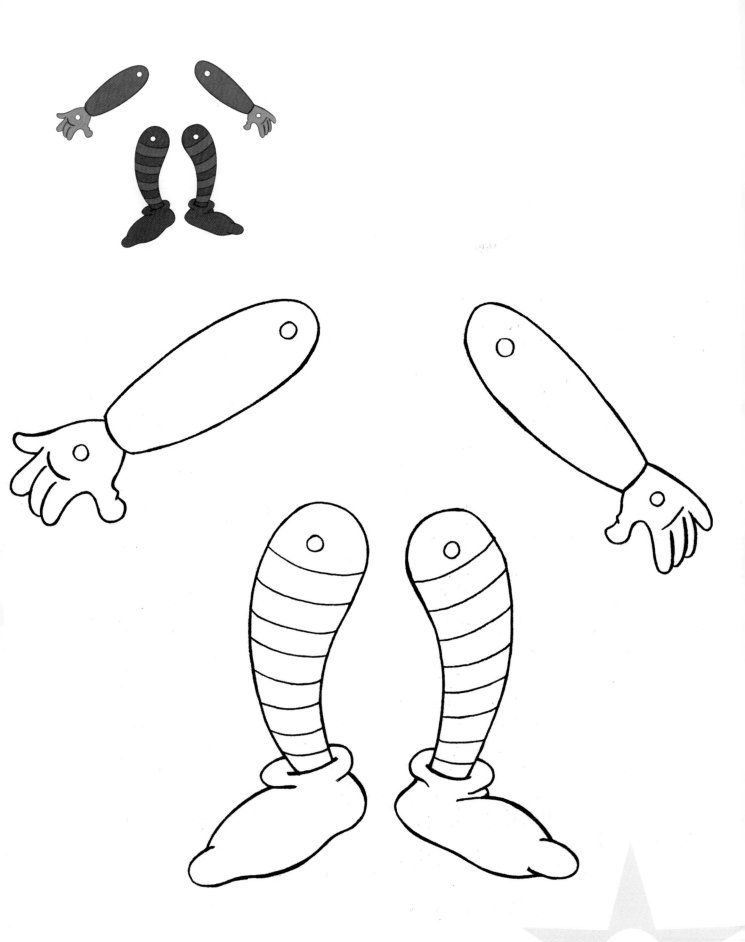

Make your own Funky Picture Frame

You Will Need

* **flour dough see pg73**

* **2 lollipop sticks**

* **Paint of assorted colours**

* **glue**

Due to all the beautiful scenery in Ireland it is a good idea to have a fun picture frame to show off some pictures or drawings.

1 Make the flour dough mix and follow instructions on page 73. You will need two lumps of dough.

2 Roll one lump into a small ball and press onto worktop. Insert a gap in the centre with a lollipop stick.

3 Now you will use the second lump of flour. Roll it out and make the shape of a shamrock, a cross or a flag.

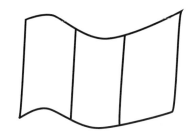

Leave in the oven for five hours at the lowest heat, to dry out. Make sure that an adult is with you to supervise this.

4 Glue the lollipop sticks together leaving a gap at the top so that the photo or picture will fit in between it. Make the front lollipop stick shorter so your photo will be supported at the back.

5 Glue your shamrock to the top of the front lollipop stick. Glue both securely into the base.

6 Now you can paint the photoframe whatever colours you like. If you have used the flag remember the colours are green, white and orange and the shamrock is green.

You can choose any picture you like in the photoframe or even a small picture you have drawn yourself.

Make your own Wind Chimes

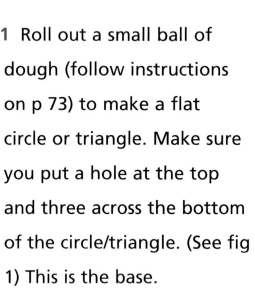

* **flour dough**
* **3 Chimes (pipe)**
* **Paint**
* **String**

With the mild breeze blowing it might be nice to have the music of wind chimes....

1 Roll out a small ball of dough (follow instructions on p 73) to make a flat circle or triangle. Make sure you put a hole at the top and three across the bottom of the circle/triangle. (See fig 1) This is the base.

2 You can again use a shamrock, cross or flag (see P. 71) at the front of the design and glue to the base.

3 Paint all the pieces bright colours. Allow to dry.

4 Glue the pieces on top of each other and allow to dry. Varnish to finish.

5 Then put the chimes below and above the design with string. It is nice to use a bead at the top for a pretty finish.

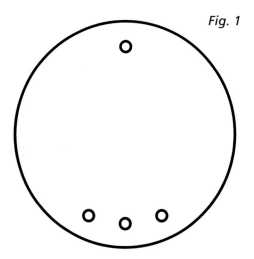

Fig. 1

Well done. You now have a chime that will play music in the wind.

Flour Dough Mix

1 Mix salt, flour and cooking oil in a bowl. Add a little water until you have a smooth paste.

2 Shake a little flour onto a worktop. Roll the dough onto it with a rolling pin.

3 Your dough is ready to use. You can now make any shape or design you like.

4 You leave the shape at the very lowest heat in the oven for five hours. Make sure you have an adult with you to check that everything is safe.

5 When they are cooked the shapes will go hard. Leave on a tray and allow to cool.

6 Paint your masterpiece whatever colour you like.

7 You must be sure to varnish the dough. This is to make it durable and last a long time.

We used our flour dough on lots of our craft ideas - our picture frame base, our jewellery tree base and our wind chime. It can also be used for lots of other ideas of your own. Experiment and have fun.

By using the flour dough to make beads you can make very pretty jewellery.

Weaving - an old traditional craft

A long time ago in Ireland back in the iron age, people used to weave on a loom. You needed some wool going in a downwards direction and you would simply weave in and out the vertical strands, across the loom. You could make cloth, blankets, clothes or whatever people needed. Machines have now taken the place of many hand weaving techniques as hand weaving can take time to complete.

It is still possible to buy some woven scarfs and blankets today which are very beautiful.

You can make some
hand woven items yourself!

Weave your own Table Mat

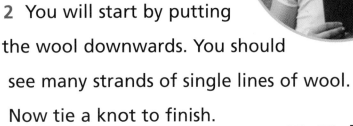

1 Cut out the following shape in card. Make them large enough for your mat. (fig1)

2 You will start by putting the wool downwards. You should see many strands of single lines of wool. Now tie a knot to finish.

You Will Need

* **Wool**

* **thick card**

* **scissors**

3 Now use a different colour and start at the top. Tie a knot to secure.

Fig. 1

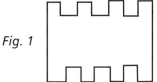

4 Move the wool in and out of the vertical strands one direction. When you reach the end of the line you move back in the opposite direction. Keep weaving in and out of the vertical strands. Patience, this takes a long time!!

5 You can use as many colours as you like. Each time you use another colour you must tie a knot to secure at the beginning and end of your work. When you are finished you can cut the wool across the back from the downward strands of wool. Gather a few pieces together and neatly tie them in a knot. Do this at both ends. This will give it a nice finish.

Well done. You have now made your own table mat to put on the kitchen table!

Make your own AIB Money Box

You Will Need

* coloured pipe cleaners
* small container with lid (cylinder shape)
* acryllic Paints
* newspaper,
* wallpaper paste
* glue
* sellotape
* flour dough mix

Make the flour dough and follow instructions from page 73.

1 Use the flour dough mix to make the shape of simple shoes. Place a small gap where the legs will fit in.

2 Glue some colourful pipecleaners in the shoes. Allow to dry. Paint the shoes whatever colour you like. Use a little piece of pipecleaner as shoelaces. This is not essential but it looks good. Try it.

3 Sellotape these colourful pipecleaners to the bottom of the cylinder shape for legs.

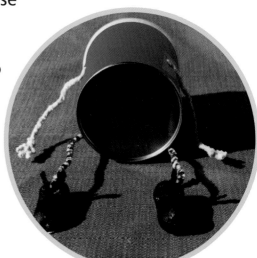

4 Make some arms and hands by twisting pink pipecleaners around the bottom of another pink pipecleaner. Now sellotape these to the sides of the cylinder shape.

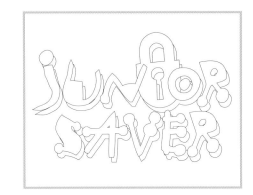

5 Now copy or trace the following face. Glue this onto card. Sellotape this onto the top of the cylinder shape.

6 Now put the wallpaper paste onto newspaper and cover the entire cylinder shape with a thin layer of newspaper. Allow to dry.

7 When it is dry you can paint this whatever colour you like.

8 Trace or copy the Junior Saver logo. Colour this with colouring markers.

9 Now cut it in a circular shape and glue it to the front of your money box.

Well done, you have now made your own Junior Saver money box. You can put coins or notes into it to keep them safe.

Acknowledgements

Little bits of Ireland has been an accumulation of so many artistic, amazing people and I am indebted to them all. Firstly to the animated characters created by Stella Kearns who has been so much fun and so positive to work with. To Jackie and Michélé from Crackerjack Design who came up with the colourful designs throughout and were patient and hard working to the close. To Gerry Smyth for his patience, support and his endless passion for photography.

To Denise O'Grady who guided and supported me on some of the more difficult days, thanks. To John for his solid advice and support. To the editing skills and late nights from Jackaline Duignan and Aisling O'Grady. To Paul and Orla for always taking an interest and ready to be an ear at the end of the phone line. To Denis and Pauline for their strength, their belief and love. To Dave for installing the washing machine!

To Trevor and the Danker crew who are always so helpful and encouraging along the way. To Mary O'Reilly from Duchas for her welcoming, warm nature and for letting me view Rosgrae Castle on the quieter days. To Tom and John for helping me get up that round tower in Clonmacnoise, I don't know how the monks did it.

To Tony Roache at Duchas, Mark Boyer from Christ Church and John Horgan from Shannon Development all who organised photographs within the book. For the background artwork from Dave Nolan on pages 29-30. To Declan for his help with the finished craft photography. To Sean and Cormac at Lafayette Photography for the kind use of the studio. To all at John Gunne Photography.

THANKS!!

To all the LCC crew for the use of their grounds and to my pupils who gave me their encouragement and support.
To Gert and Jackie for brainstorming! For the encouragement and advice from Therese Hackett and Denise Kennedy. To Billy for friendship, contracts and tea!

To all the kids who were so willing and helpful to experiment with crafts and were so photo friendly. To Patsy Kavanagh, the Kaye family, and all the kids at Michael's Light.

To AnnMarie Frayne and Siobhan McDonald at AIB for their professionalism, enthusiasm and belief in the book. Lets hope you were right! To all those people out there who buy it, thanks for the support! Enjoy!